THE BIG FEARON BOOK OF
Math·A·Draw

PRIMARY LEVEL
Addition & Subtraction for Grades K–4

81 dot-to-dot math learning games
sequenced according to level of difficulty

Judith N. Parsons

MAKEMASTER® Blackline Masters
Fearon Teacher Aids
a division of
PITMAN LEARNING, INC.
Belmont, California

Entire contents copyright © 1984 by Pitman Learning, Inc.,
19 Davis Drive, Belmont, California 94002. Member of the Pitman Group.
Permission is hereby granted to reproduce designated materials in this book
for noncommercial classroom and individual use.

ISBN-0-8224-4559-X

Printed in the United States of America.

1.9 8 7 6 5 4 3 2 1

Preface

The Big Fearon Book of Math-A-Draw, Primary Level has been specially created to provide you with materials of exceptional educational value in a convenient package. Since we felt that teachers everywhere would like to have as many books as possible from our <u>brand</u> <u>new</u> Math-A-Draw series, we decided to gather three of the Primary Level books from the series together under one cover. The three books included in *The Big Fearon Book of Math-A-Draw* offer more than 80 addition and subtraction exercises that are carefully sequenced for maximum learning value. Each exercise provides both practice and review as well as a motivating dot-to-dot art activity. The materials in this book cover enough skill development levels to give you a wealth of exercises for a wide range of student abilities. We hope that the Math-A-Draw activities in this Big Book format will prove beneficial to both you and your students.

Three Intermediate Level books, covering multiplication and division, are also available in the convenient Big Book format.

Introduction

Math-A-Draw Primary Level materials have been thoroughly classroom tested and used with success to supplement math texts for students in kindergarten through fourth grade. Most teachers find that students need considerably more practice with basic math skills than is provided in the standard texts. Math-A-Draw materials are designed to provide both this practice and the all-important motivation for students to "stick with it" until they have mastered the skill involved. Most teachers will agree that it's easy to provide problems for practice but much harder to provide effective motivation. Math-A-Draw meets this critical need in several ways.

The Big Fearon Book of Math-A-Draw—Primary Level contains 81 problem sets. Each set includes an A and a B worksheet. The A worksheet provides basic addition and subtraction problems to be solved by your students. The B worksheet provides a dot-to-dot activity containing a hidden picture.

Your students will work and solve the problems on worksheet A and then use their answers, in order, to connect the dots on worksheet B. As they connect the dots, the hidden picture emerges to surprise and delight them. An answer key is provided in the back of the book so that you may check students' work easily or so that the students may check their own answers.

A record card is provided so that you can monitor each student's progress through the Math-A-Draw sequence. A certificate of congratulations is also included. This may be awarded to each student as he or she successfully completes the *Math-A-Draw Level I*, *Level II*, or *Level III* materials.

Math-A-Draw Primary Level materials are ideal companions to kindergarten through fourth grade math texts. For example, after each math concept has been taught, the corresponding Math-A-Draw activities will provide highly motivating practice. Problem sets are carefully sequenced to provide practice reinforcement for each step in learning math concepts and skills.

For students, connecting the dots to find the hidden picture and coloring the completed drawings provide an incentive to solve the problems correctly and move on to new material. Solving an arithmetic problem and then using the answer to create a picture reinforces many additional skills: identifying numbers, following directions, understanding spatial relationships, sequencing, and so on. Literally having something to show for their work ensures students a high level of motivation and imparts a sense of closure.

How to Use Math-A-Draw as a Class Activity

Follow these steps to introduce Math-A-Draw to your class:

1. Reproduce the A and B worksheets for Set 1 for each student. Be sure to reproduce extra B worksheets, as some students like to start over if they make a mistake.

2. Pass out the A worksheets. Keep the B worksheets at your desk. (When the B worksheets are passed out with the A worksheets, students may try to guess at the picture and then use the numbers from worksheet B as answers to worksheet A's problems.)

3. Have the students work all the problems on worksheet A. Ask them to work rapidly but carefully. Explain that they will need to have *all* the answers right in order to find the hidden picture, which you will pass out in a few minutes.

4. Check the answers. It is important that answers be checked as soon as possible after the student has finished solving the problems so that excitement about doing worksheet B does not dissipate. You, the student, or another student may check the answers. If a student has done more than two problems incorrectly, have him or her try to solve those problems again. Be sure that each student has all the answers on worksheet A right, even if you do not have her or him redo any problems. Do not pass out worksheet B until you are sure that all problems have been checked and the correct answers have been written on worksheet A.

5. Pass out worksheet B. In subsequent lessons, worksheet B may be given to individual students as soon as they complete worksheet A and their answers have been checked. Seeing another student trying to find the hidden picture is often a strong incentive for a student to finish his or her worksheet.

6. Be sure that all students have both the completed and checked worksheet A and worksheet B directly in front of them.

7. Say, "Look at worksheet B. Put your pencil on the dot with the arrow. This is where you will start every time you do a Math-A-Draw picture. Notice that the number next to the dot with the arrow is the same as the answer to problem 1A on worksheet A. Now look at the answer to problem 1B. Put your finger just below this answer. Now look at worksheet B and find the dot with the same number next to it. Draw a line from the dot with the arrow to this dot. Now look at worksheet A again. Find the answer to problem 1C. Find the dot on worksheet B with that number. Draw a line from the second dot to this one. Do the rest of the dot-to-dot picture in the same way. Every dot on worksheet B has a number, and each number matches an answer on worksheet A. Be sure to read the answers on worksheet A in order. If you have any trouble, raise your hand, and I'll come help you."

8. Pass out crayons or colored pencils and let students color their completed drawings.

Useful Tips

1. Here's an effective way to explain Math-A-Draw to your students:
   a. Copy the problems in Figure 1 on the left side of the chalkboard.
   b. Copy the incomplete dot-to-dot drawing (Figure 2) on the right side of the board.
   c. Solve the math problems with your students.
   d. Show the students how to use the math answers to connect the dots in proper sequence, and complete the drawing (Figure 3).

2. Make copies of the Math-A-Draw record card to keep track of student progress. Make a record card for each student in your class. You will probably find it easiest to keep the record cards

Figure 1

1. $3 + 3 = \boxed{6}$ 6. $2 + 2 = \boxed{4}$
2. $1 + 3 = \boxed{4}$ 7. $4 + 3 = \boxed{7}$
3. $3 + 2 = \boxed{5}$ 8. $7 + 1 = \boxed{8}$
4. $0 + 1 = \boxed{1}$ 9. $1 + 1 = \boxed{2}$
5. $8 + 1 = \boxed{9}$ 10. $0 + 3 = \boxed{3}$

Figure 2   **Figure 3**

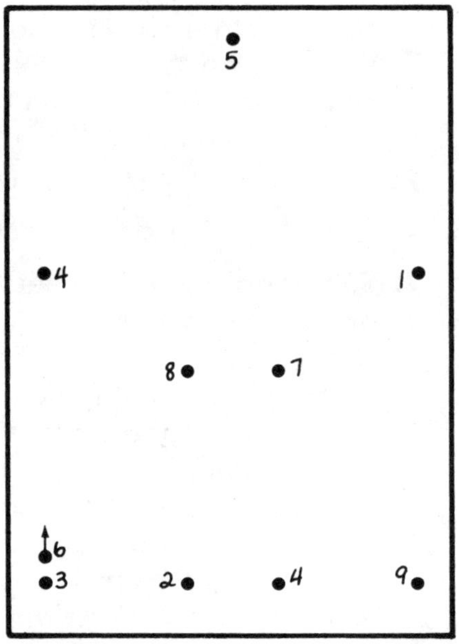

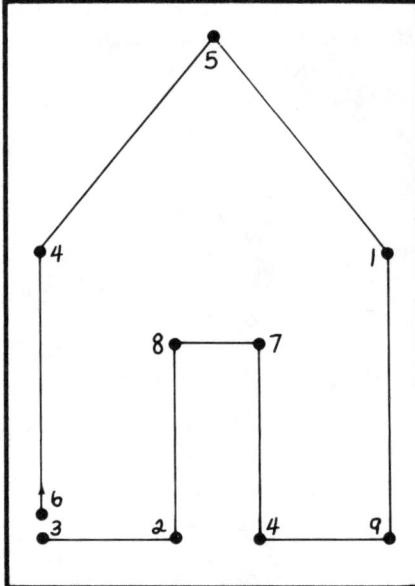

in your desk, as some students tend to lose them when they have to keep them over a period of weeks. However, you may wish to give the students envelopes and ask them to keep the record cards in their own desks or in a central file. As students finish the Math-A-Draw exercises, you may wish to indicate progress by using a hole punch to punch a hole by the completed set number (students love to do this themselves) or by marking the appropriate circle with a crayon or colored pen to indicate how well the student has done. For example, for excellent work, color the circle red; for satisfactory work, green; for unsatisfactory work, blue. After the students have completed all the Math-A-Draw sets, award copies of the Math-A-Draw Certificate to those whose work has been satisfactory to excellent.

Math·A·Draw

Level I · Addition and Subtraction for Grades K–2

27 dot-to-dot math learning games sequenced according to level of difficulty

Contents

Introduction

Record Card and Certificate

Addition with sums to 10   Sets **1–6**

Subtraction from 10   Sets **7–9**

Addition with sums to 20   Set **10**

What comes between? —Recognizing numerals in order from 1 to 20   Set **11**

What comes after? —Recognizing numerals in order from 0 to 20   Set **12**

What comes before? —Recognizing numerals in order from 0 to 20   Set **13**

Which is greater? —Numerals to 20   Set **14**

Which is smaller? —Numerals to 20   Set **15**

Addition with a constant addend   Sets **16–23**

Balancing an equation using 10 as a constant   Set **24**

Mixed addition and subtraction with sums to 20   Sets **25** and **26**

Addition with three addends and sums to 20   Set **27**

Answer Key

Math-A-Draw Level I

Name _____ Set **1** Worksheet **A**

Write the correct numeral in each box.

$3 + 2 = \square$

$2 + 2 = \square$

$5 + 2 = \square$

$2 + 1 = \square$

$5 + 5 = \square$

$3 + 5 = \square$

$1 + 0 = \square$

$3 + 3 = \square$

$4 + 5 = \square$

$1 + 1 = \square$

Math-A-Draw Level I

Name _____   Set **1** Worksheet **B**

To find the hidden picture, draw lines from dot to dot. Follow the order of your answers. Start from the dot with the arrow.

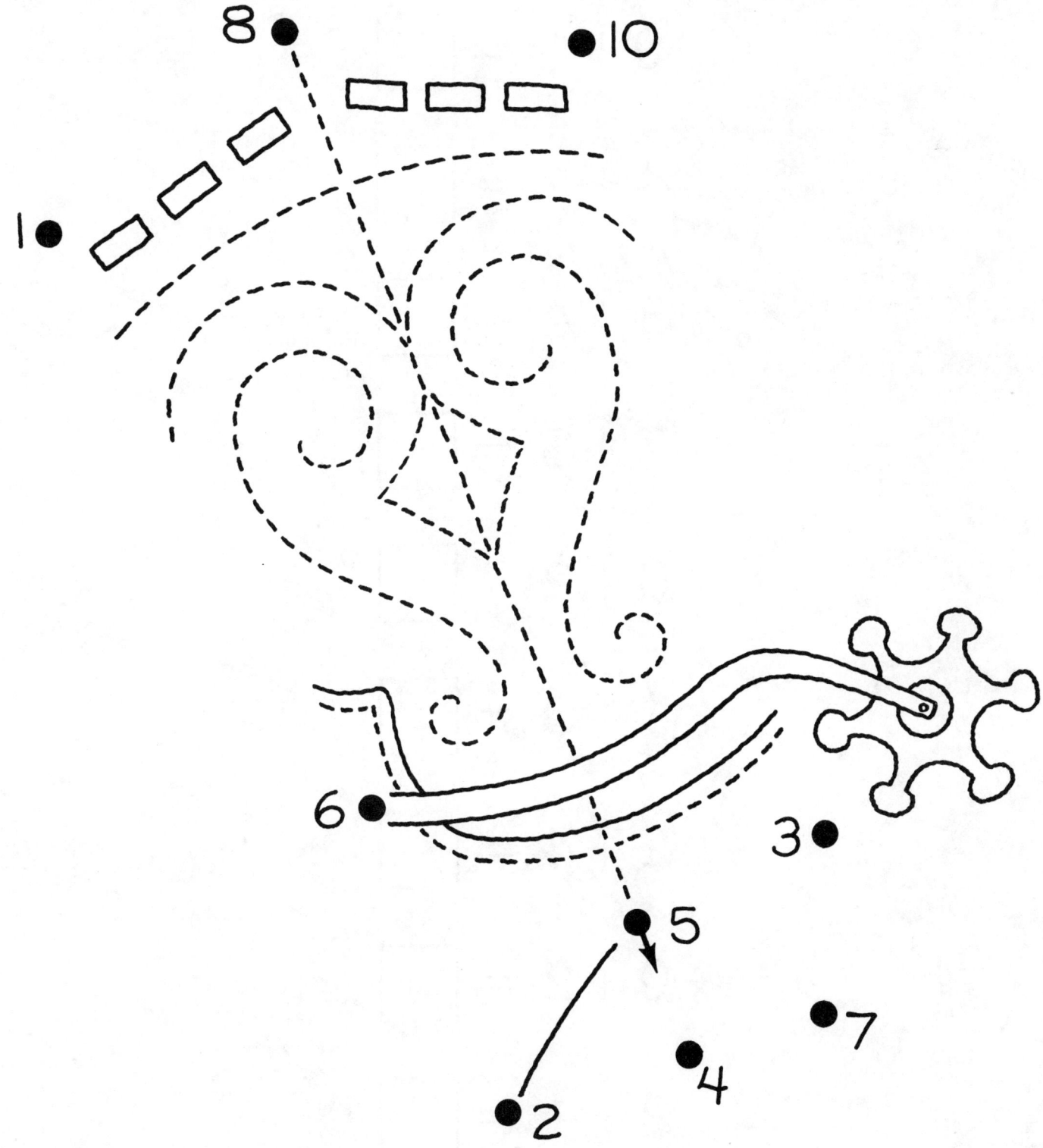

Math-A-Draw Level 1

Name _____ Set **2** Worksheet **A**

Write the correct numeral in each box.

0 + 1 = ☐

4 + 1 = ☐

3 + 4 = ☐

7 + 3 = ☐

0 + 2 = ☐

1 + 3 = ☐

2 + 4 = ☐

6 + 2 = ☐

2 + 1 = ☐

3 + 6 = ☐

Math-A-Draw Level I

Name _____ Set **2** Worksheet **B**

To find the hidden picture, draw lines from dot to dot. Follow the order of your answers. Start from the dot with the arrow.

Math-A-Draw Level I

Name _____   Set **3** Worksheet **A**

Write the correct numeral in each box.

$3 + 2 + 4 =$ ☐

$0 + 1 + 0 =$ ☐

$2 + 3 + 2 =$ ☐

$1 + 2 + 1 =$ ☐

$4 + 3 + 3 =$ ☐

$1 + 0 + 1 =$ ☐

$3 + 2 + 1 =$ ☐

$1 + 2 + 5 =$ ☐

$1 + 1 + 1 =$ ☐

$2 + 1 + 2 =$ ☐

Math-A-Draw Level I

Name _____ Set **3** Worksheet **B**

To find the hidden picture, draw lines from dot to dot. Follow the order of your answers. Start from the dot with the arrow.

Math-A-Draw Level I

Name _____ Set **4** Worksheet **A**

Write the correct numeral in each box.

$7 + \square = 10$

$0 + \square = 10$

$5 + \square = 10$

$9 + \square = 10$

$2 + \square = 10$

$4 + \square = 10$

$8 + \square = 10$

$3 + \square = 10$

$1 + \square = 10$

$6 + \square = 10$

Math-A-Draw Level I

Name _____ Set **4** Worksheet **B**

To find the hidden picture, draw lines from dot to dot. Follow the order of your answers. Start from the dot with the arrow.

Math-A-Draw Level I

Name _____ Set 5 Worksheet A

Write the correct numeral in each box.

☐ + 1 = 10

☐ + 4 = 10

☐ + 7 = 10

☐ + 2 = 10

☐ + 5 = 10

☐ + 8 = 10

☐ + 3 = 10

☐ + 6 = 10

☐ + 9 = 10

☐ + 0 = 10

Math-A-Draw Level I

Name _____ Set **5** Worksheet **B**

To find the hidden picture, draw lines from dot to dot. Follow the order of your answers. Start from the dot with the arrow.

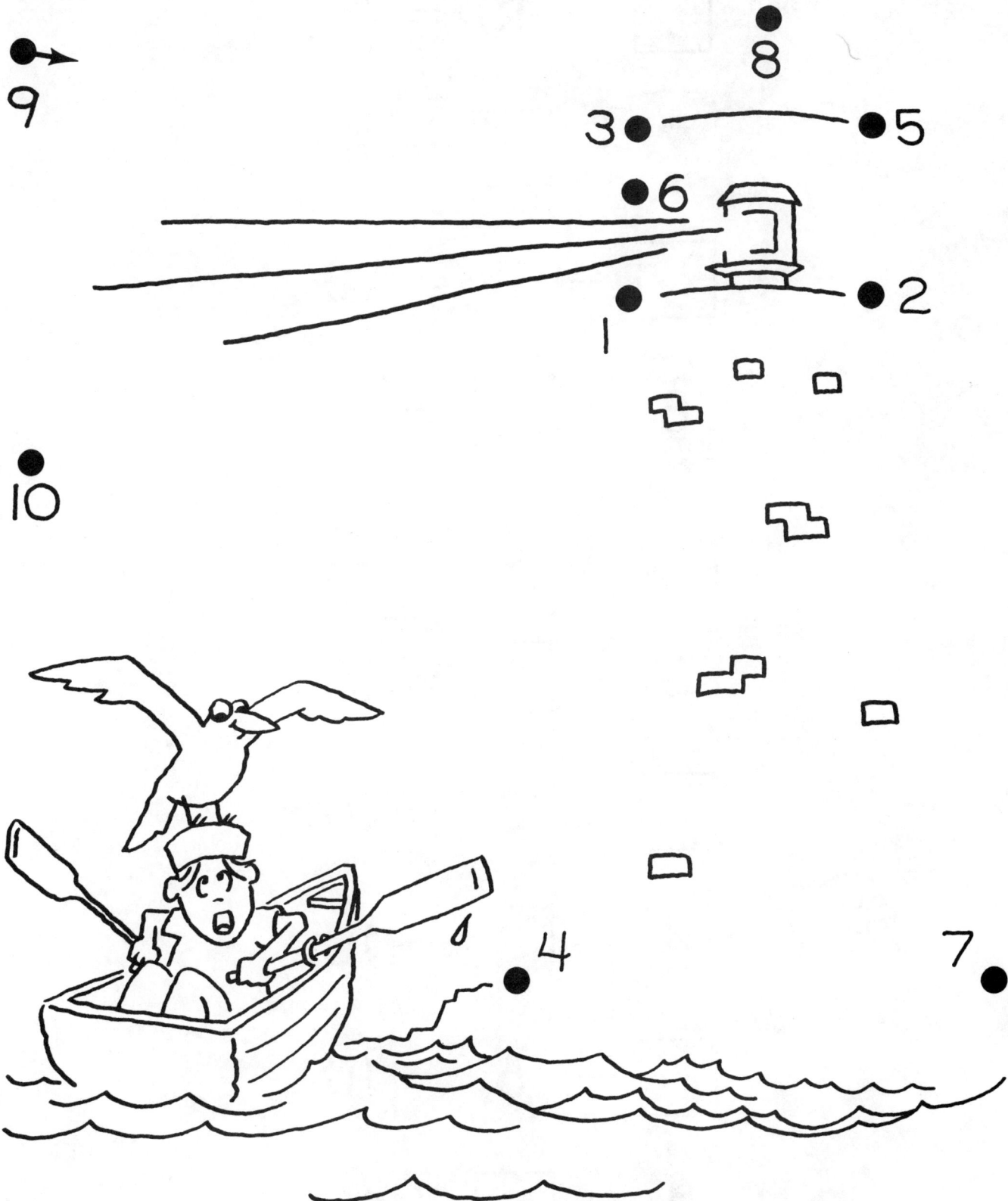

Math-A-Draw Level I

Name _____ Set **6** Worksheet **A**

Write the correct numeral in each box.

☐ + 10 = 10

7 + ☐ = 10

☐ + 9 = 10

6 + ☐ = 10

☐ + 8 = 10

3 + ☐ = 10

☐ + 2 = 10

4 + ☐ = 10

☐ + 5 = 10

1 + ☐ = 10

Math-A-Draw Level I

Name _____ Set **6** Worksheet **B**

To find the hidden picture, draw lines from dot to dot. Follow the order of your answers. Start from the dot with the arrow.

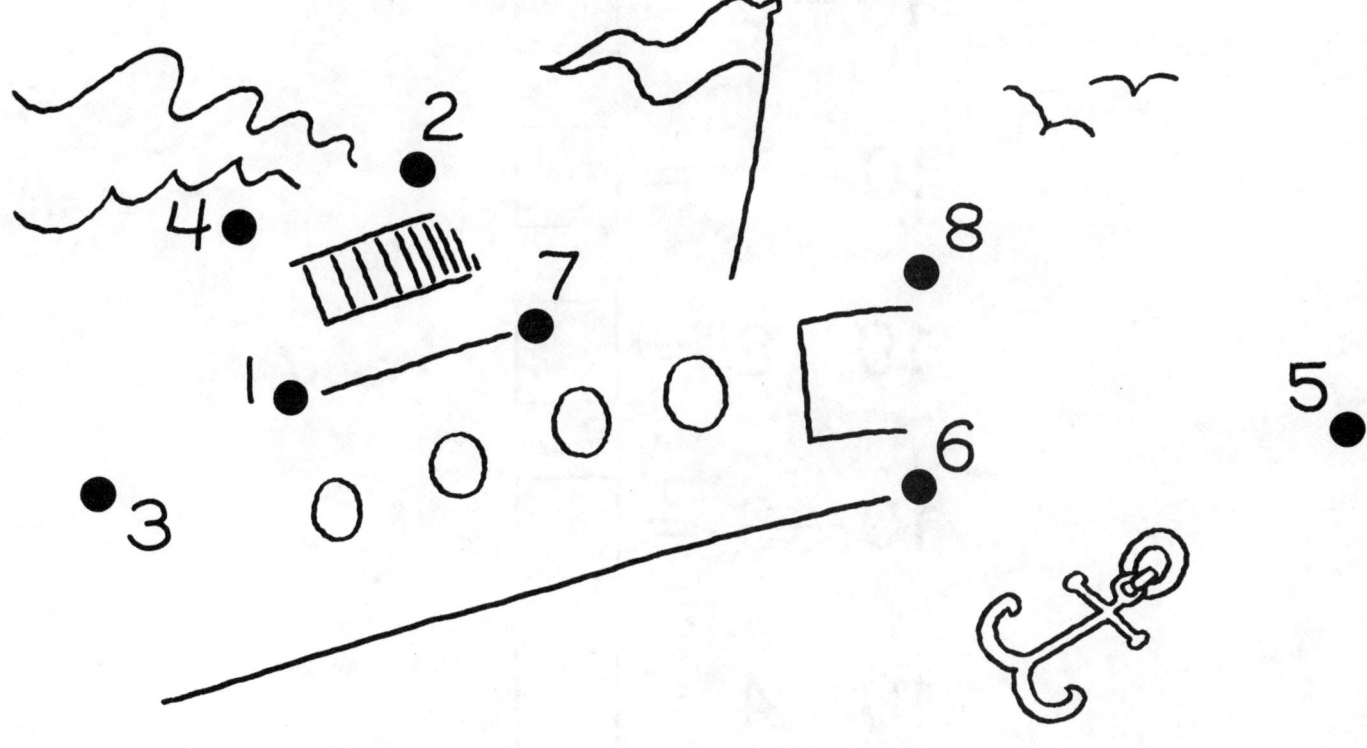

Math-A-Draw Level I

Name _____ Set 7 Worksheet **A**

Write the correct numeral in each box.

10 − 5 = ☐

10 − 7 = ☐

10 − 2 = ☐

10 − 9 = ☐

10 − 4 = ☐

10 − 0 = ☐

10 − 3 = ☐

10 − 6 = ☐

10 − 1 = ☐

10 − 8 = ☐

Math-A-Draw Level I

Name _____ Set **7** Worksheet **B**

To find the hidden picture, draw lines from dot to dot. Follow the order of your answers. Start from the dot with the arrow.

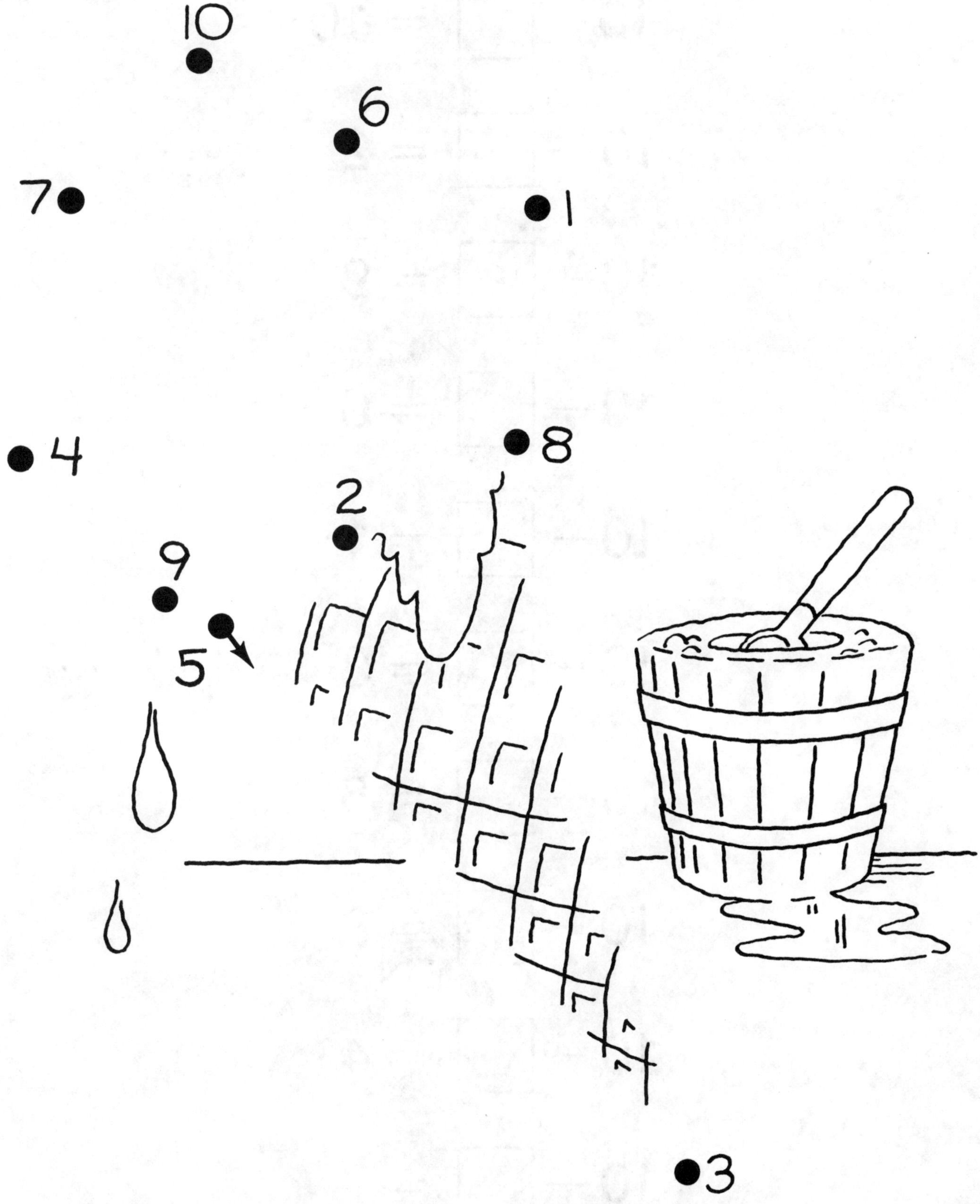

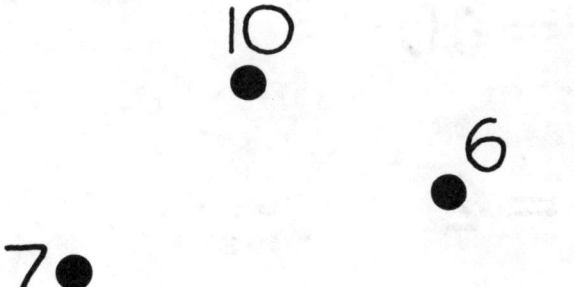

Math-A-Draw Level I

Name _____ Set **8** Worksheet **A**

Write the correct numeral in each box.

$10 - \square = 10$

$10 - \square = 2$

$10 - \square = 9$

$10 - \square = 6$

$10 - \square = 1$

$10 - \square = 3$

$10 - \square = 5$

$10 - \square = 8$

$10 - \square = 4$

$10 - \square = 7$

Math-A-Draw Level I

Name _____ Set **8** Worksheet **B**

To find the hidden picture, draw lines from dot to dot. Follow the order of your answers. Start from the dot with the arrow.

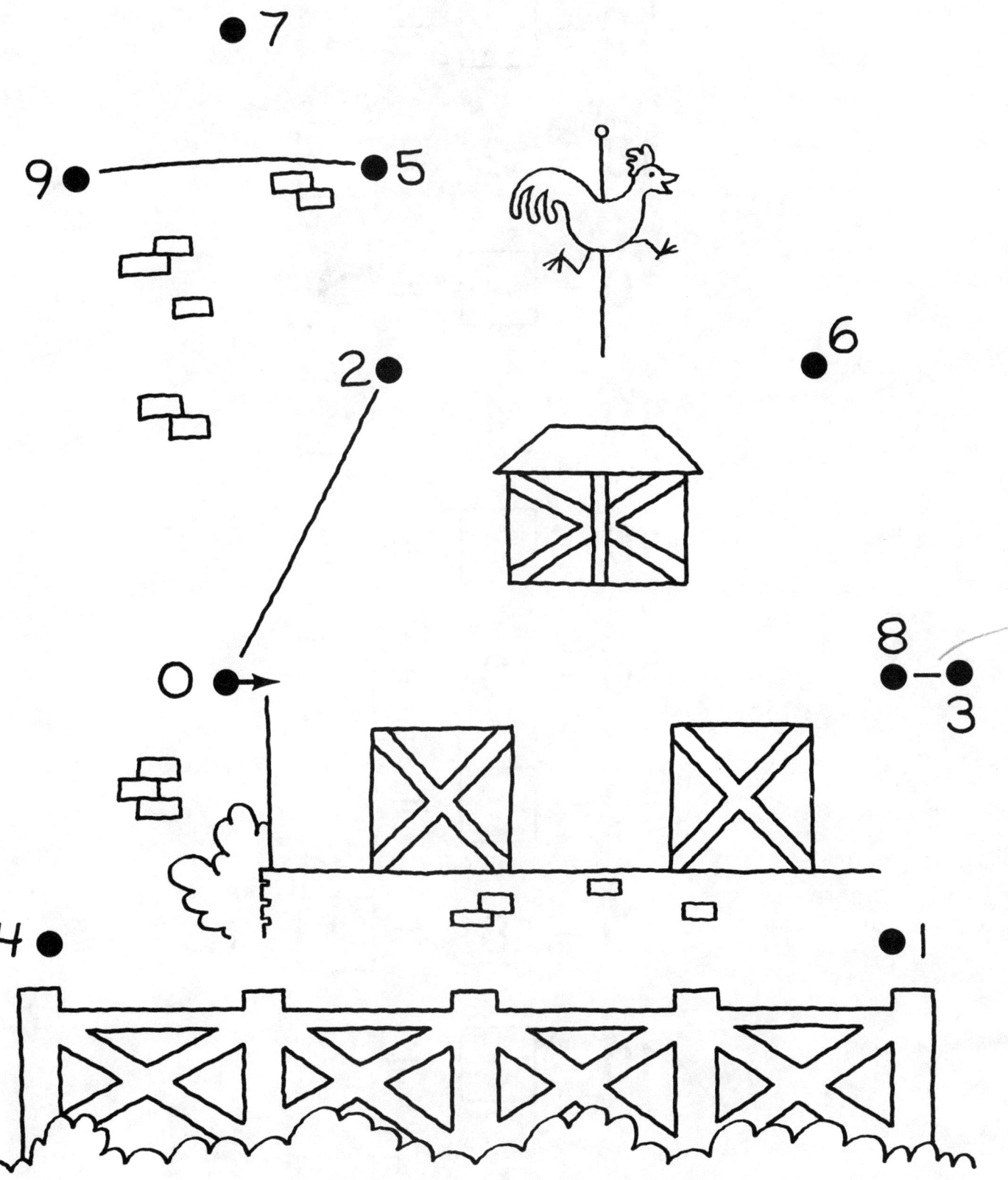

Math-A-Draw Level I

Name _____ Set **9** Worksheet **A**

Write the correct numeral in each box.

10 − ☐ = 1

10 − 2 = ☐

10 − ☐ = 3

10 − 4 = ☐

10 − ☐ = 9

10 − 0 = ☐

10 − ☐ = 7

10 − 8 = ☐

10 − ☐ = 5

10 − 6 = ☐

Math-A-Draw Level I

Name _____   Set **9** Worksheet **B**

To find the hidden picture, draw lines from dot to dot. Follow the order of your answers. Start from the dot with the arrow.

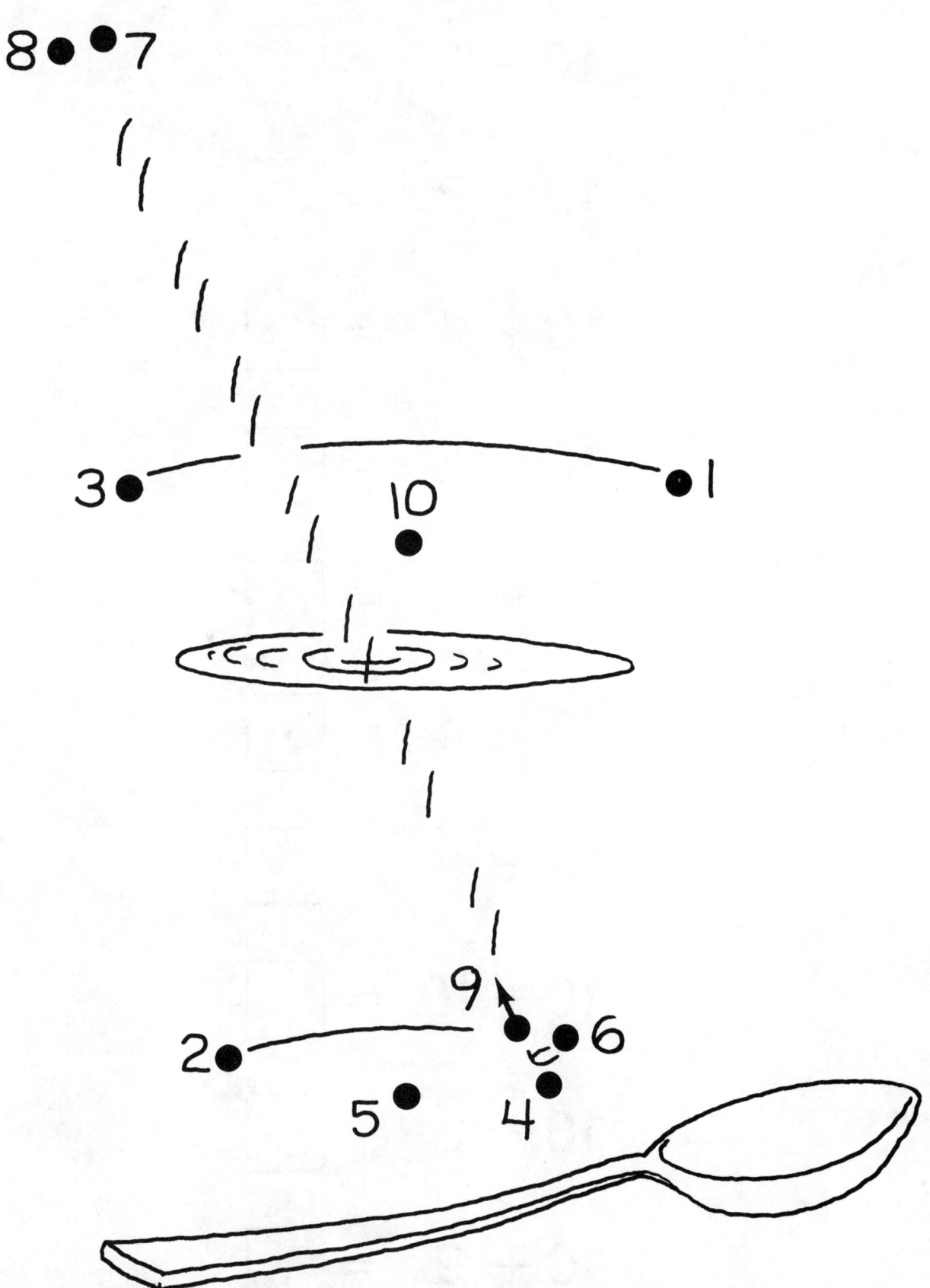

Math-A-Draw Level I

Name _____   Set **10** Worksheet **A**

Write the correct numeral in each box.

$10 + 2 = \square$

$10 + 7 = \square$

$10 + 1 = \square$

$10 + 5 = \square$

$10 + 8 = \square$

$10 + 4 = \square$

$10 + 6 = \square$

$10 + 10 = \square$

$10 + 3 = \square$

$10 + 9 = \square$

Math-A-Draw Level I

Name _____ Set 10 Worksheet **B**

To find the hidden picture, draw lines from dot to dot. Follow the order of your answers. Start from the dot with the arrow.

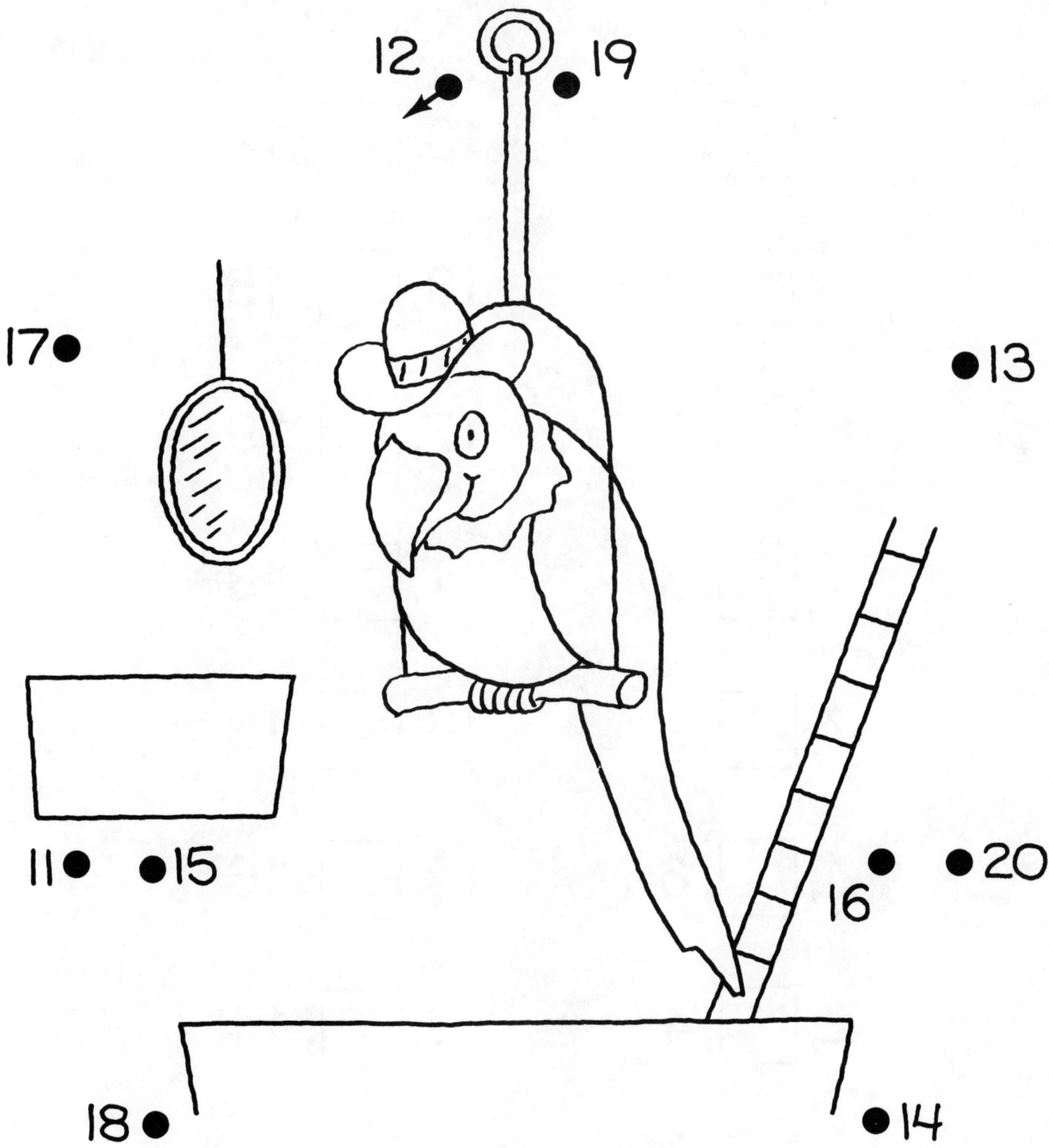

Math-A-Draw Level I

Name _____ Set **11** Worksheet **A**

What comes between? Write the missing numeral in each box.

5, ☐, 7   15, ☐, 17

3, ☐, 5   10, ☐, 12

8, ☐, 10   13, ☐, 15

6, ☐, 8   17, ☐, 19

1, ☐, 3   11, ☐, 13

7, ☐, 9   16, ☐, 18

4, ☐, 6   14, ☐, 16

2, ☐, 4   12, ☐, 14

9, ☐, 11   18, ☐, 20

Math-A-Draw Level I

Name _____ Set **11** Worksheet **B**

To find the hidden picture, draw lines from dot to dot. Follow the order of your answers. Start from the dot with the arrow.

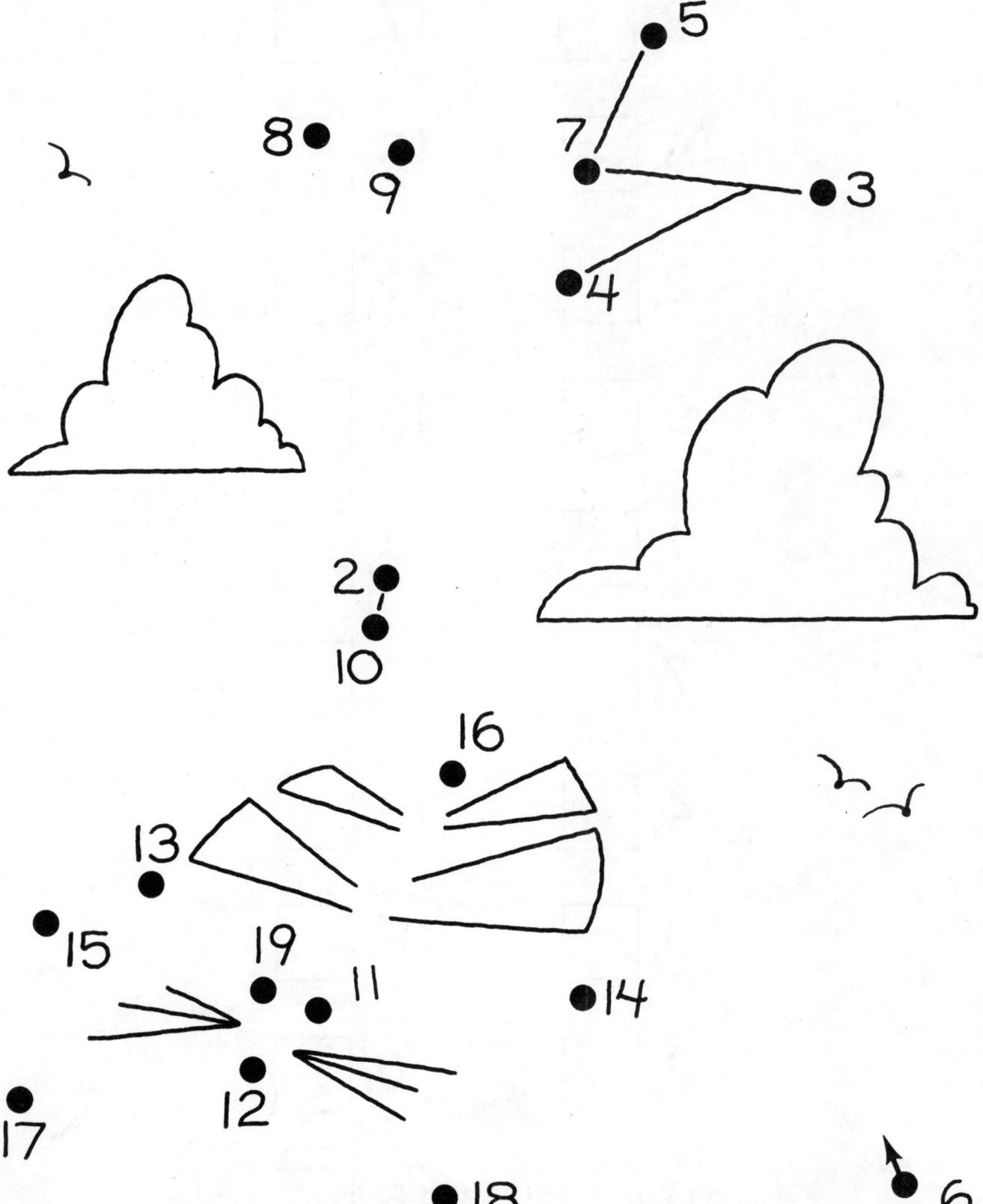

Math-A-Draw Level I

Name _____ Set **12** Worksheet **A**

What comes after? Write the missing numeral in each box.

8, ☐   17, ☐

5, ☐   13, ☐

2, ☐   11, ☐

9, ☐   18, ☐

1, ☐   14, ☐

7, ☐   12, ☐

4, ☐   19, ☐

6, ☐   16, ☐

3, ☐   0, ☐

10, ☐   15, ☐

Math-A-Draw Level I

Name _____ Set **12** Worksheet **B**

To find the hidden picture, draw lines from dot to dot. Follow the order of your answers. Start from the dot with the arrow.

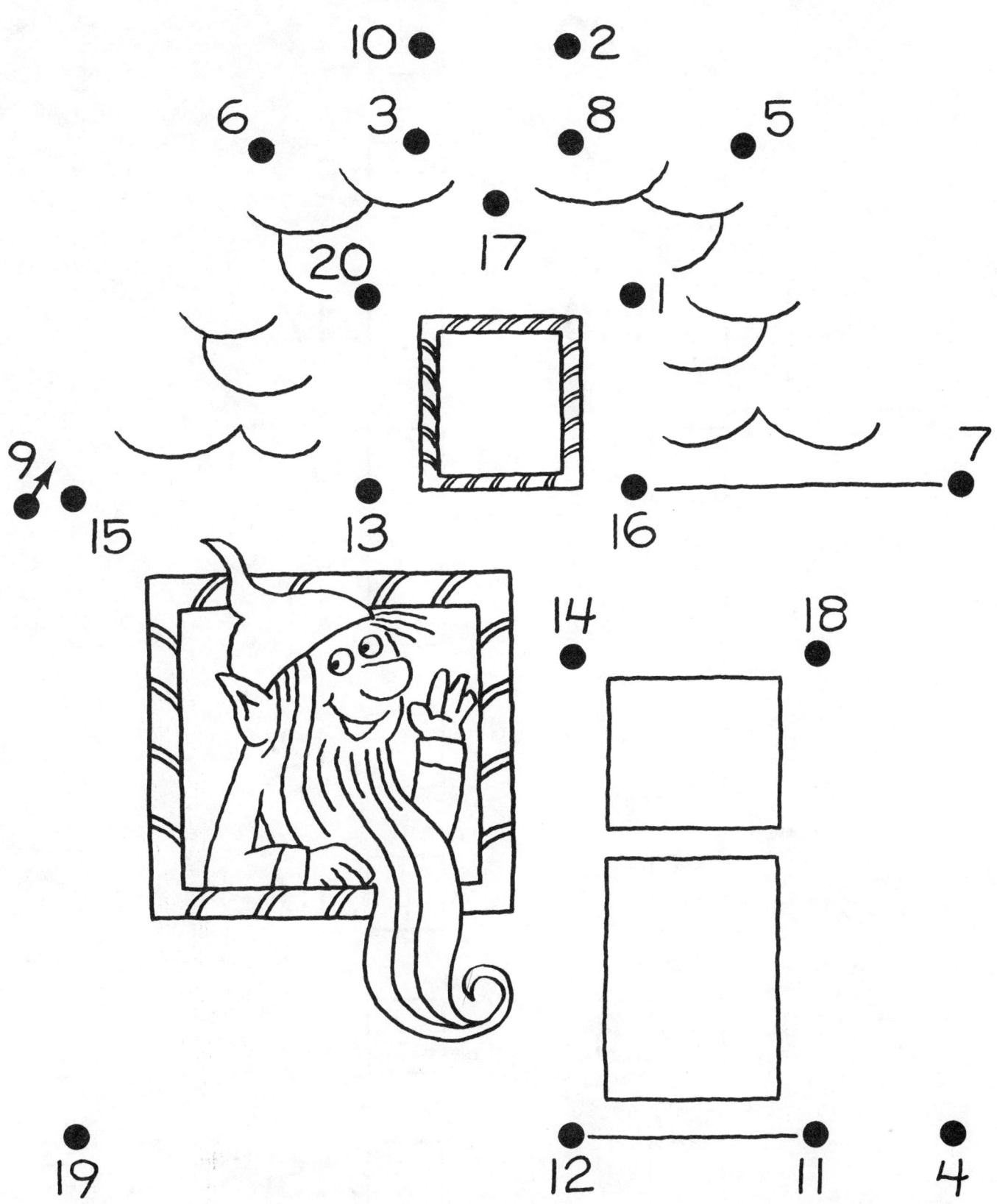

Math-A-Draw Level I

Name _____ Set **13** Worksheet **A**

What comes before? Write the missing numeral in each box.

☐, 20   ☐, 11

☐, 9   ☐, 8

☐, 16   ☐, 17

☐, 5   ☐, 3

☐, 10   ☐, 14

☐, 13   ☐, 12

☐, 18   ☐, 19

☐, 6   ☐, 7

☐, 4   ☐, 15

Math-A-Draw Level I

Name _____ Set **13** Worksheet **B**

To find the hidden picture, draw lines from dot to dot. Follow the order of your answers. Start from the dot with the arrow.

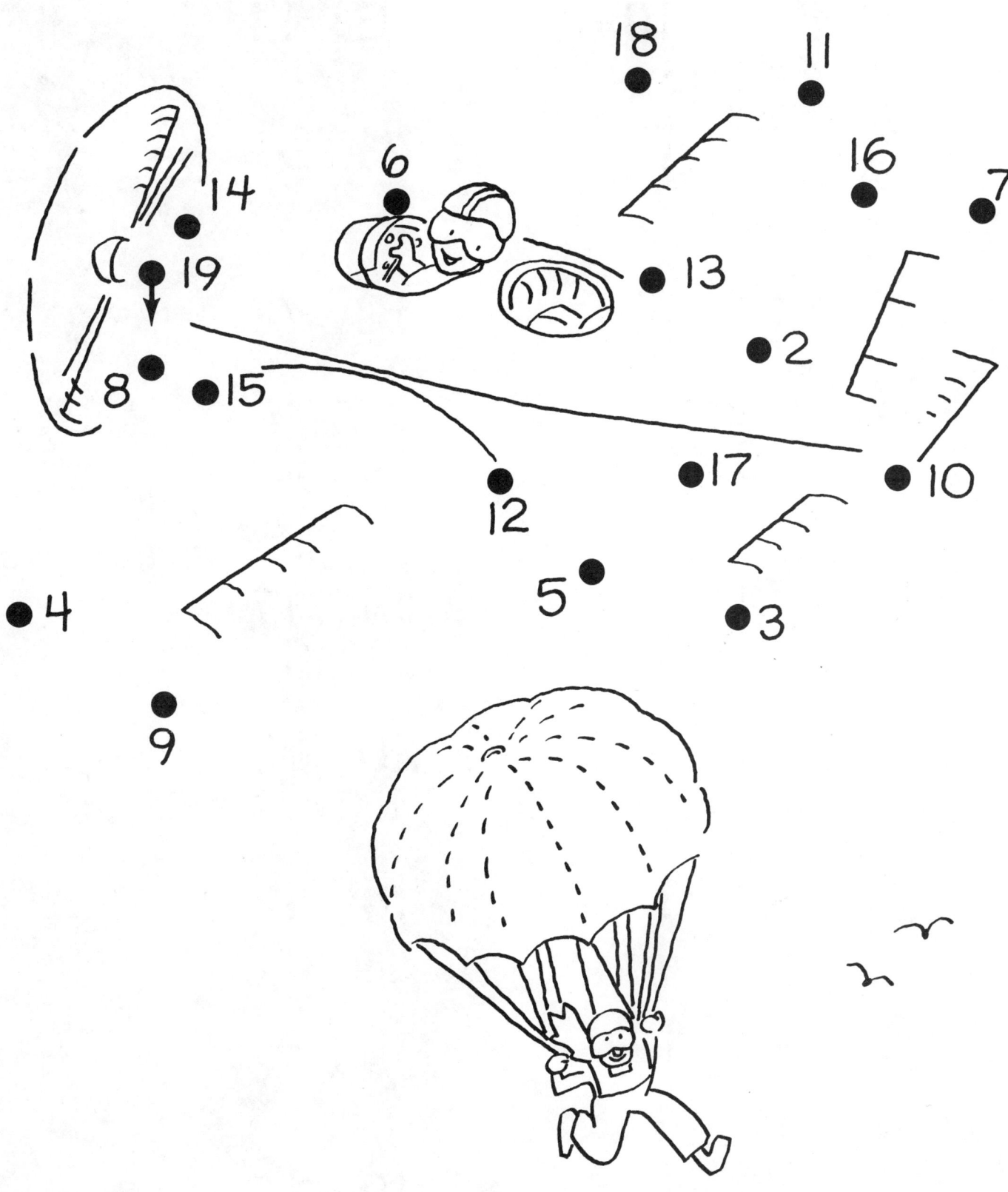

Math-A-Draw Level I

Name _____ Set **14** Worksheet **A**

Circle the numeral that is greater in each pair.

8, 10	8, 11
2, 4	2, 3
12, 16	12, 7
9, 5	6, 2
13, 11	14, 17
14, 18	20, 15
7, 3	14, 12
15, 12	6, 8
3, 5	19, 17

Math-A-Draw Level I

Name _____ Set **14** Worksheet **B**

To find the hidden picture, draw lines from dot to dot. Follow the order of your answers. Start from the dot with the arrow.

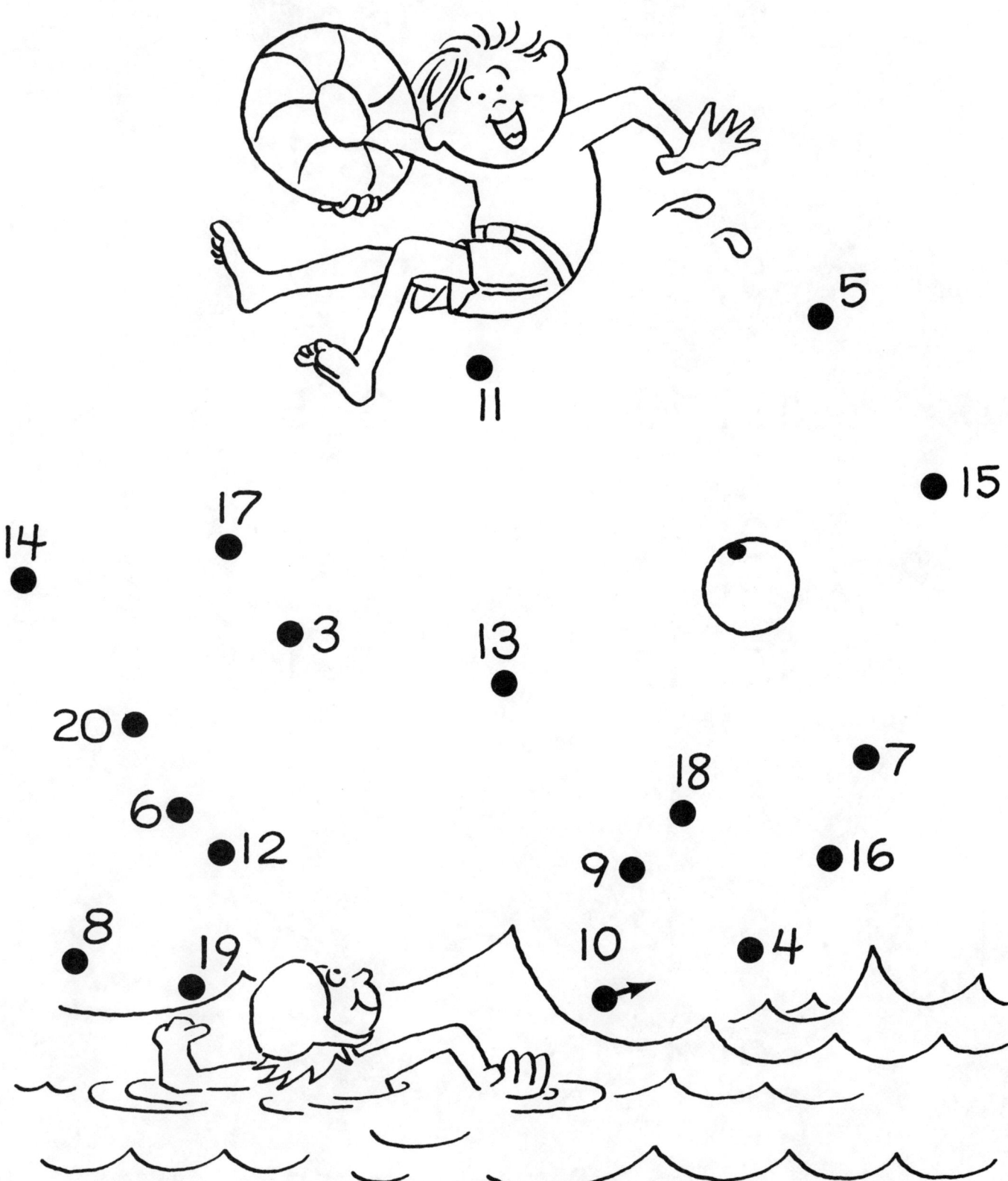

Math-A-Draw Level I

Name _____ Set **15** Worksheet **A**

Circle the numeral that is smaller in each pair.

20, ▼18   16, ▼17

13, 10   13, 18

5, 8   12, 7

12, 15   3, 5

9, 6   19, 20

15, 17   14, 18

8, 11   13, 11

9, 12   17, 20

6, 4   2, 8

             1, 5

Math-A-Draw Level I

Name _____ Set **15** Worksheet **B**

To find the hidden picture, draw lines from dot to dot. Follow the order of your answers. Start from the dot with the arrow.

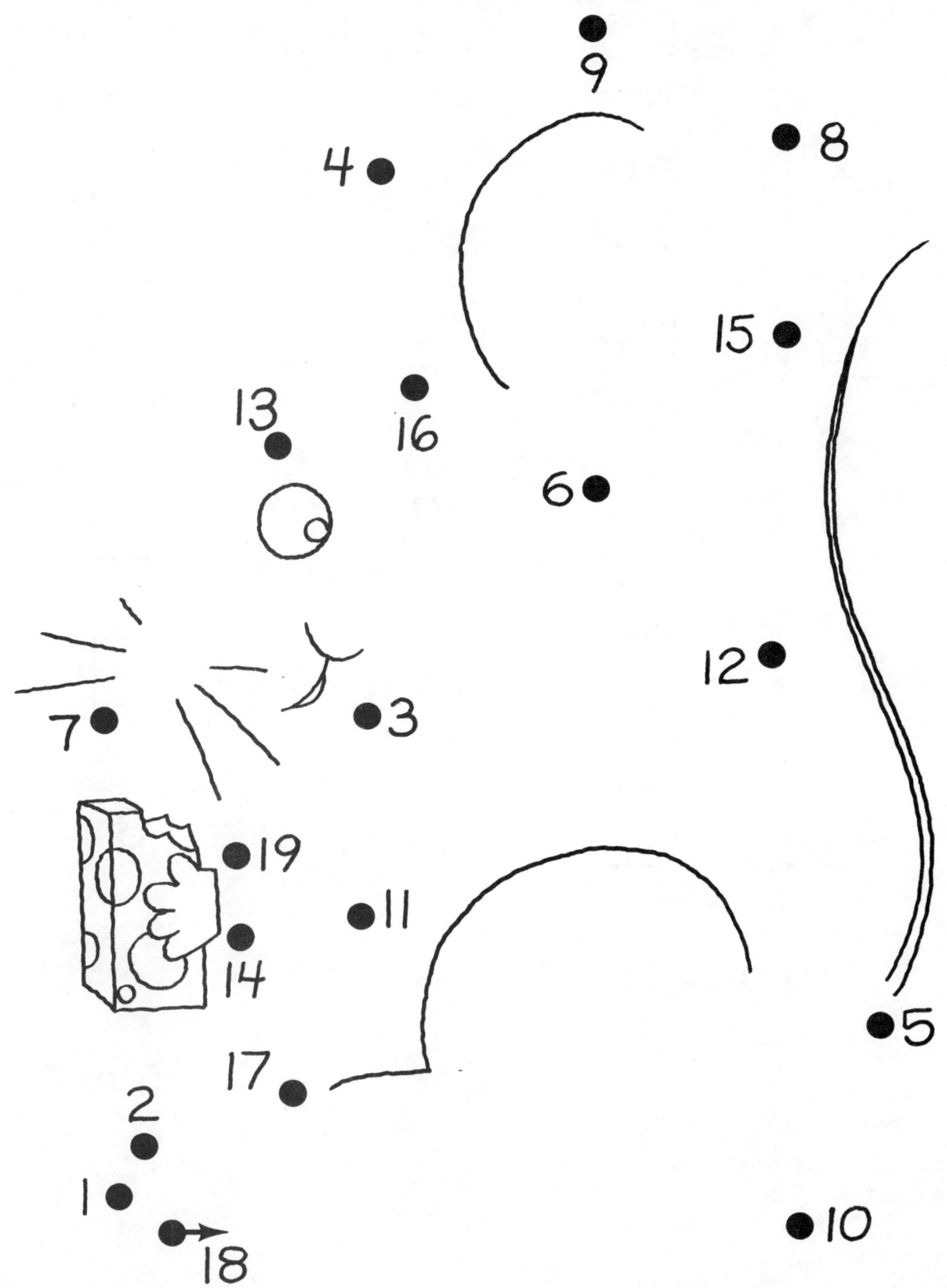

Math-A-Draw Level I

Name _____ Set **16** Worksheet **A**

Write the correct numeral in each box.

2 + 3 = ☐   2 + 6 = ☐

2 + 8 = ☐   2 + 1 = ☐

2 + 0 = ☐   2 + 5 = ☐

2 + 9 = ☐   2 + 10 = ☐

2 + 7 = ☐   2 + 4 = ☐

2 + 2 = ☐   2 + ☐ = 3

Math-A-Draw Level I

Name _____   Set **16** Worksheet **B**

To find the hidden picture, draw lines from dot to dot. Follow the order of your answers. Start from the dot with the arrow.

Math-A-Draw Level I

Name _____   Set **17**   Worksheet **A**

Write the correct numeral in each box.

3 + 3 = ☐   3 + 6 = ☐

3 + 8 = ☐   3 + 4 = ☐

3 + 2 = ☐   3 + 10 = ☐

3 + 7 = ☐   3 + 5 = ☐

3 + 1 = ☐   3 + ☐ = 5

3 + 9 = ☐   3 + ☐ = 4

3 + 0 = ☐

Math-A-Draw Level I

Name _____   Set **17** Worksheet **B**

To find the hidden picture, draw lines from dot to dot. Follow the order of your answers. Start from the dot with the arrow.

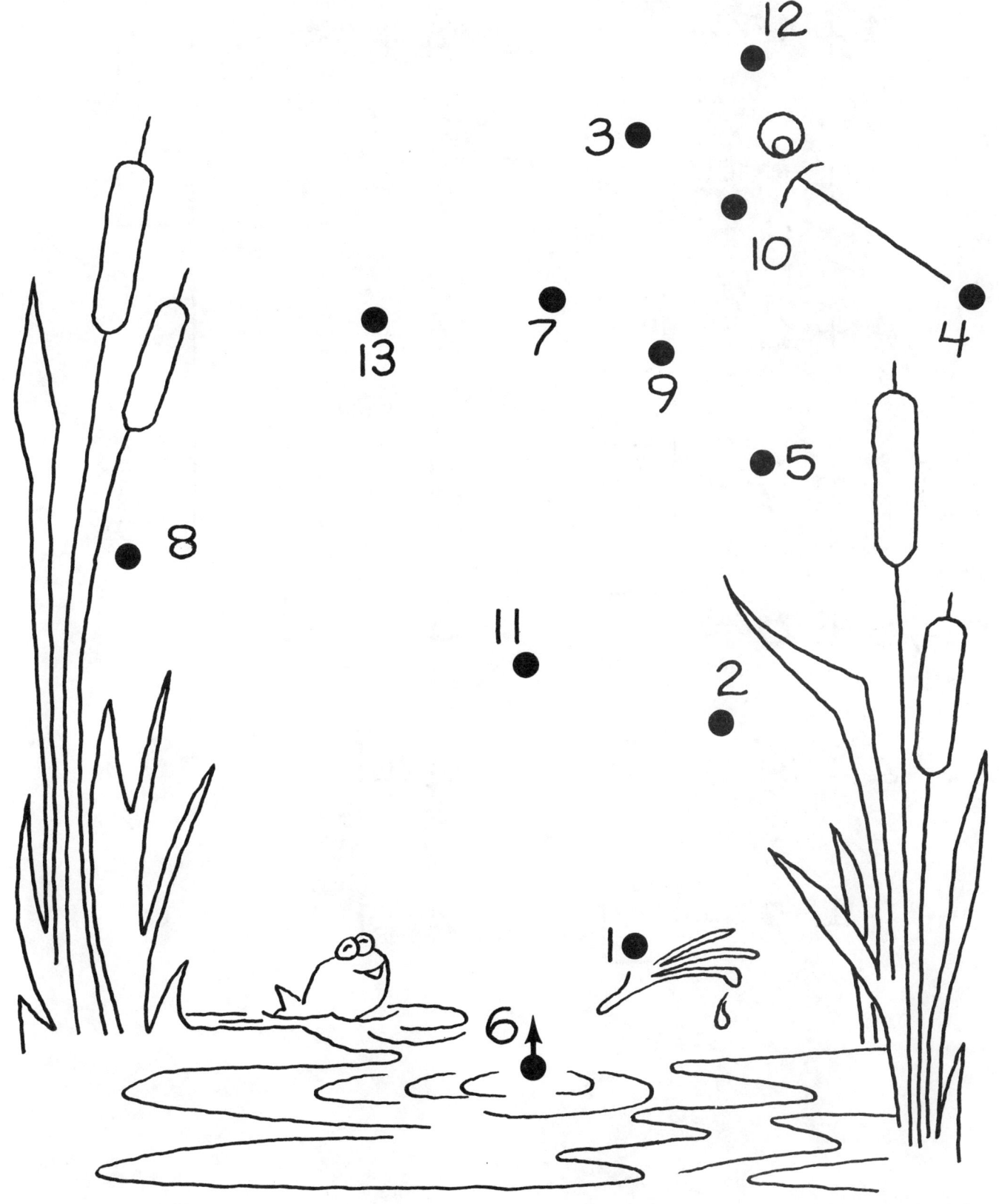

Math-A-Draw Level 1

Name _____ Set **18** Worksheet **A**

Write the correct numeral in each box.

4 + 10 = ☐   4 + 4 = ☐

4 + 6 = ☐   4 + 9 = ☐

4 + 3 = ☐   4 + 7 = ☐

4 + 0 = ☐   4 + 1 = ☐

4 + 5 = ☐   4 + ☐ = 7

4 + 8 = ☐   4 + ☐ = 5

4 + 2 = ☐   4 + ☐ = 6

Math-A-Draw Level I

Name _____   Set **18** Worksheet **B**

To find the hidden picture, draw lines from dot to dot. Follow the order of your answers. Start from the dot with the arrow.

Math-A-Draw Level I

Name _____ Set **19** Worksheet **A**

Write the correct numeral in each box.

5 + 5 = ☐   5 + 4 = ☐

5 + 9 = ☐   5 + 10 = ☐

5 + 1 = ☐   5 + 7 = ☐

5 + 6 = ☐   5 + 3 = ☐

5 + 0 = ☐   5 + ☐ = 9

5 + 8 = ☐   5 + ☐ = 7

5 + 2 = ☐   5 + ☐ = 8

Math-A-Draw Level I

Name _____   Set **19** Worksheet **B**

To find the hidden picture, draw lines from dot to dot. Follow the order of your answers. Start from the dot with the arrow.

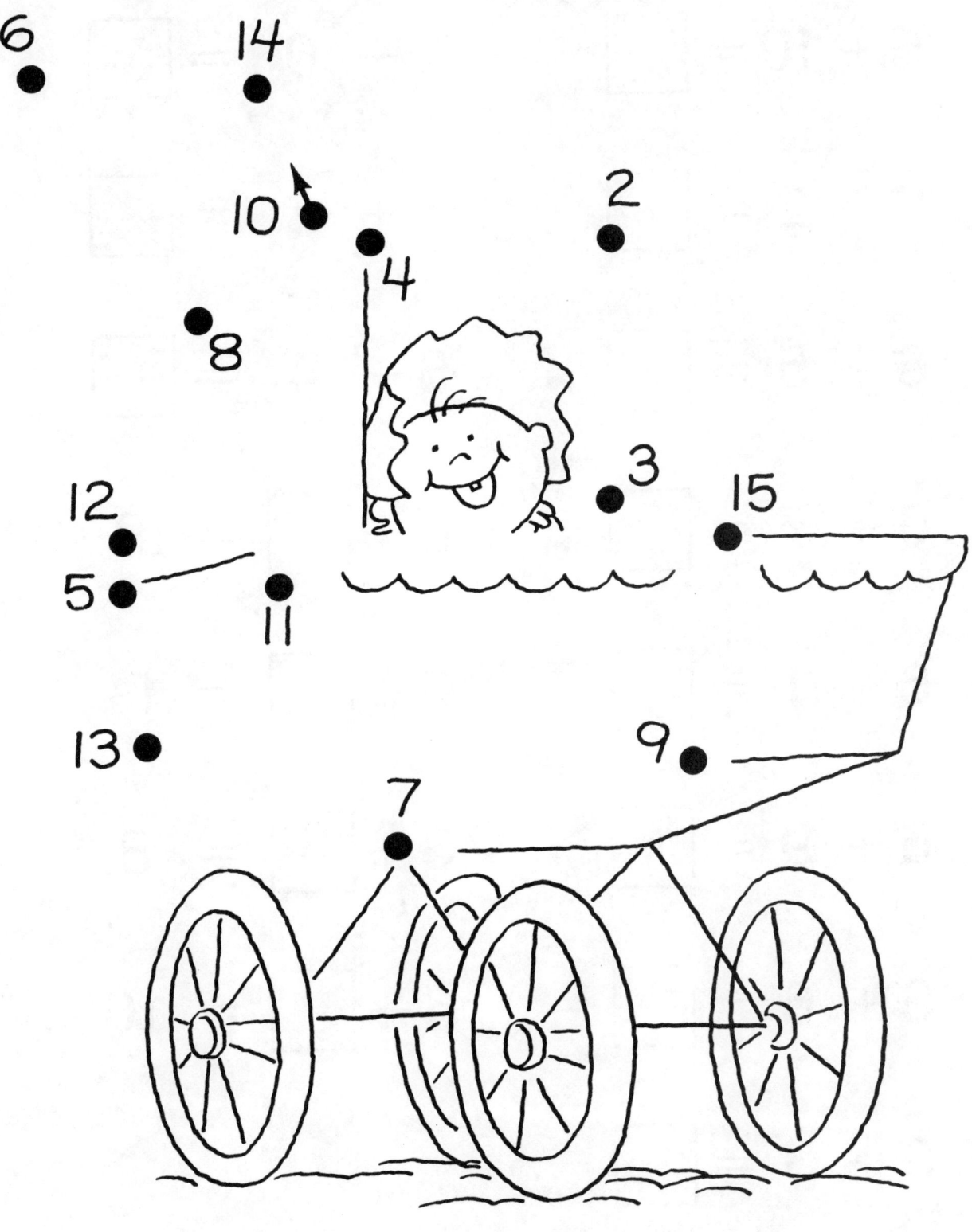

Math-A-Draw Level I

Name _____   Set **20**   Worksheet **A**

Write the correct numeral in each box.

6 + 10 = ☐   6 + 0 = ☐

6 + 2 = ☐   6 + 8 = ☐

6 + 5 = ☐   6 + 4 = ☐

6 + 7 = ☐   6 + ☐ = 9

6 + 1 = ☐   6 + ☐ = 11

6 + 9 = ☐   6 + ☐ = 8

6 + 6 = ☐   6 + ☐ = 10

6 + 3 = ☐

Math-A-Draw Level I

Name _____ Set **20** Worksheet **B**

To find the hidden picture, draw lines from dot to dot. Follow the order of your answers. Start from the dot with the arrow.

Math-A-Draw Level I

Name _____   Set **21**   Worksheet **A**

Write the correct numeral in each box.

7 + 8 = ☐   7 + 9 = ☐

7 + 3 = ☐   7 + 1 = ☐

7 + 7 = ☐   7 + 5 = ☐

7 + 4 = ☐   7 + ☐ = 10

7 + 0 = ☐   7 + ☐ = 13

7 + 6 = ☐   7 + ☐ = 11

7 + 10 = ☐   7 + ☐ = 9

7 + 2 = ☐   7 + ☐ = 12

Math-A-Draw Level I

Name _____   Set **21** Worksheet **B**

To find the hidden picture, draw lines from dot to dot. Follow the order of your answers. Start from the dot with the arrow.

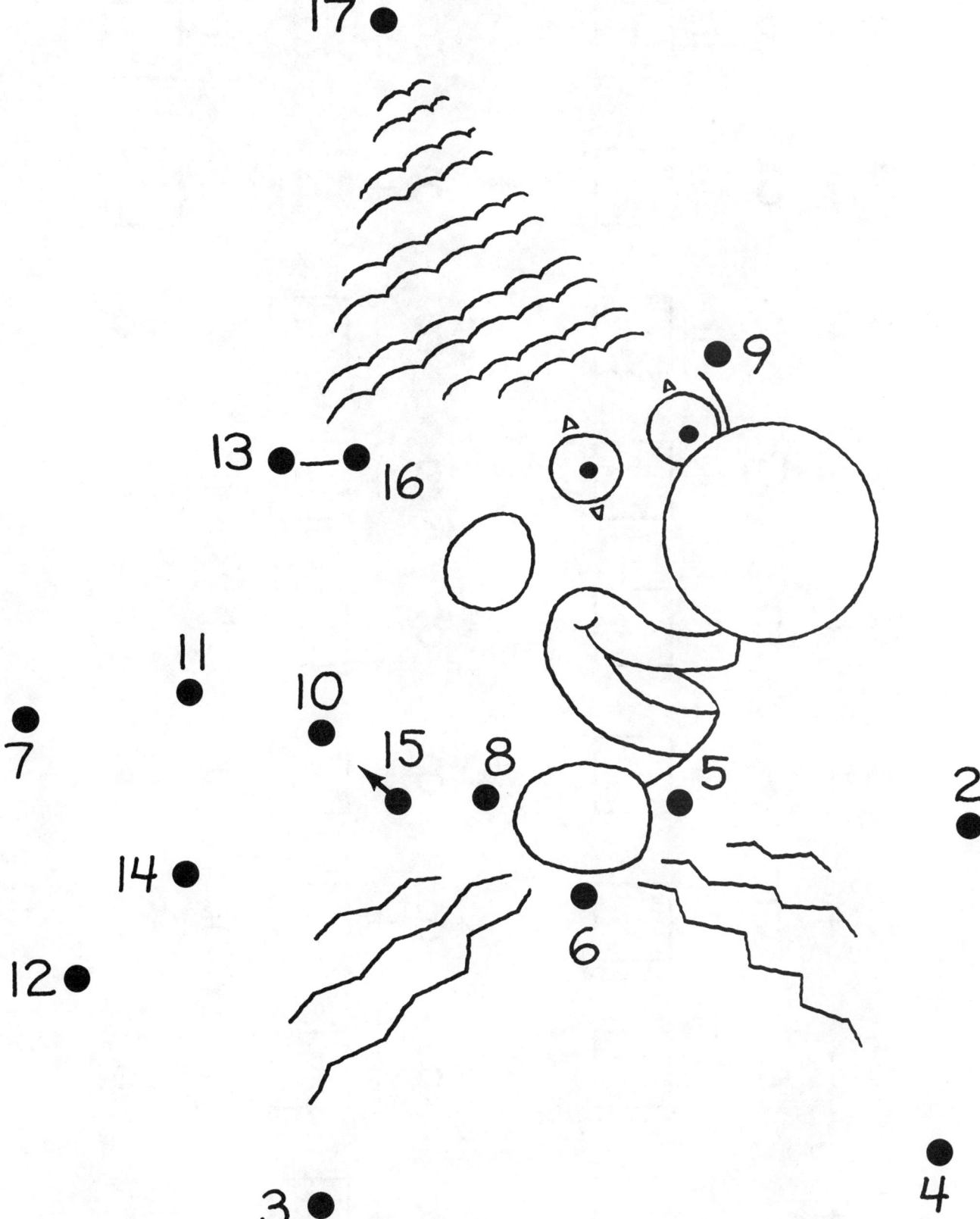

Math-A-Draw Level I

Name _____   Set **22**   Worksheet **A**

Write the correct numeral in each box.

8 + 3 = ☐   8 + 9 = ☐

8 + 6 = ☐   8 + 4 = ☐

8 + 2 = ☐   8 + ☐ = 12

8 + 10 = ☐   8 + ☐ = 10

8 + 0 = ☐   8 + ☐ = 15

8 + 7 = ☐   8 + ☐ = 14

8 + 5 = ☐   8 + ☐ = 11

8 + 8 = ☐   8 + ☐ = 13

8 + 1 = ☐   8 + ☐ = 9

Math-A-Draw Level I

Name _____ Set **22** Worksheet **B**

To find the hidden picture, draw lines from dot to dot. Follow the order of your answers. Start from the dot with the arrow.

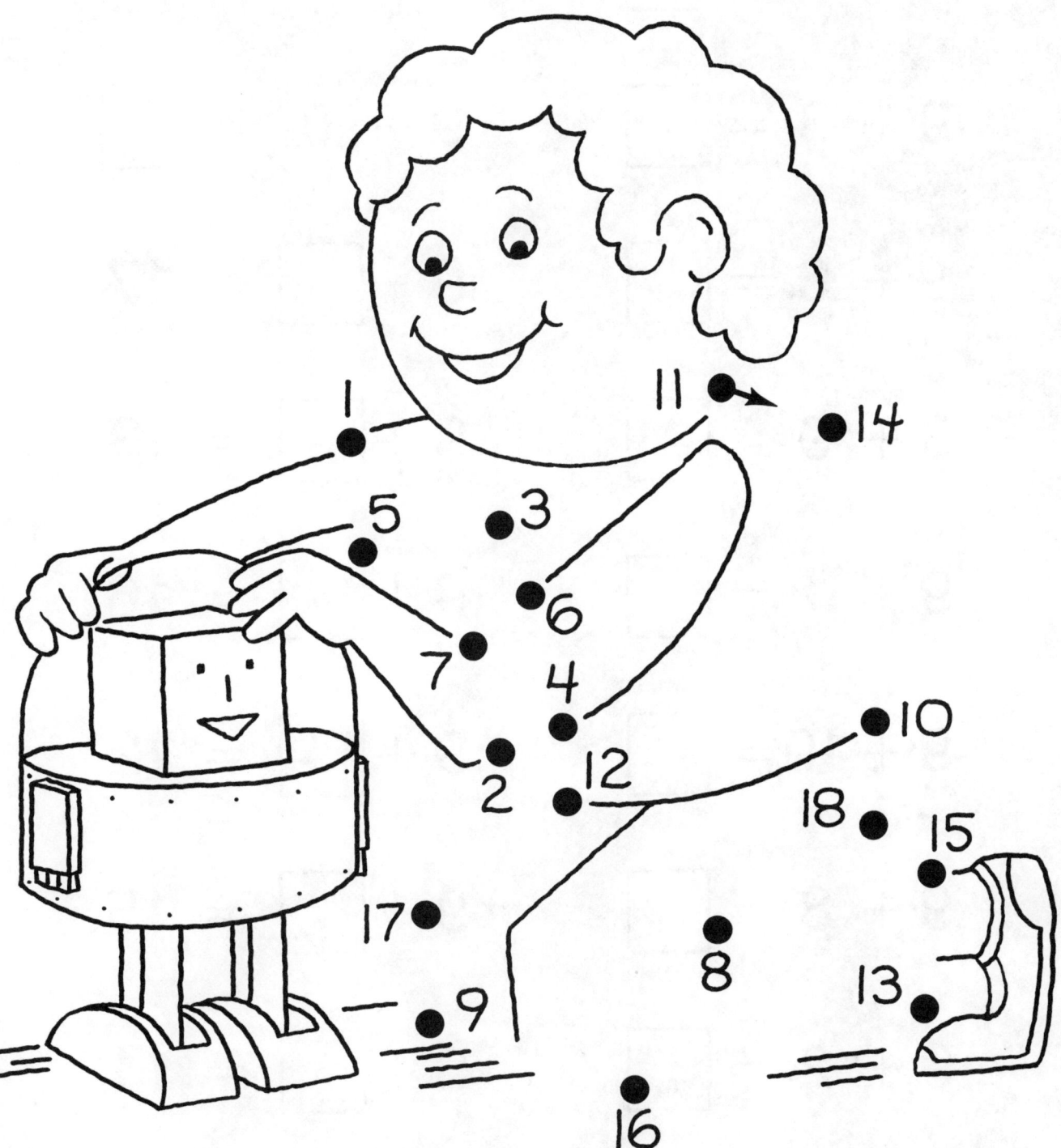

Math-A-Draw Level I

Name _____   Set **23**   Worksheet **A**

Write the correct numeral in each box.

9 + 7 = ☐   9 + 5 = ☐

9 + 3 = ☐   9 + 0 = ☐

9 + 6 = ☐   9 + ☐ = 17

9 + 9 = ☐   9 + ☐ = 13

9 + 1 = ☐   9 + ☐ = 16

9 + 10 = ☐   9 + ☐ = 12

9 + 8 = ☐   9 + ☐ = 15

9 + 2 = ☐   9 + ☐ = 11

9 + 4 = ☐   9 + ☐ = 14

Math-A-Draw Level I

Name _____ Set **23** Worksheet **B**

To find the hidden picture, draw lines from dot to dot. Follow the order of your answers. Start from the dot with the arrow.

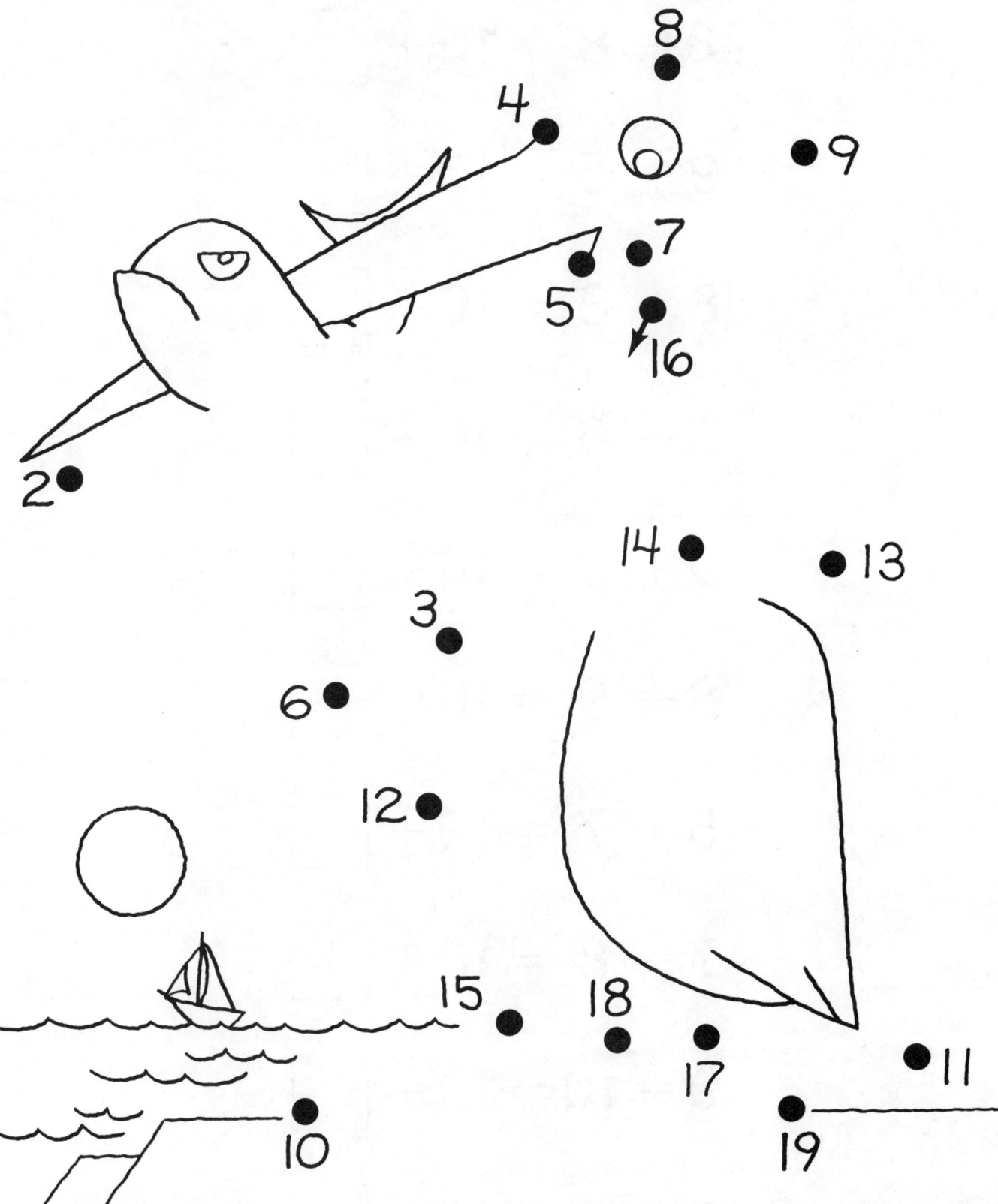

Math-A-Draw Level I

Name _____ Set **24** Worksheet **A**

Write the correct numeral in each box.

8 + 8 = 10 + ☐

9 + 5 = 10 + ☐

8 + 3 = 10 + ☐

7 + 6 = 10 + ☐

9 + 9 = 10 + ☐

8 + 9 = 10 + ☐

5 + 7 = 10 + ☐

7 + 8 = 10 + ☐

9 + 10 = 10 + ☐

5 + 5 = 10 + ☐

Math-A-Draw Level I

Name _____ Set **24** Worksheet **B**

To find the hidden picture, draw lines from dot to dot. Follow the order of your answers. Start from the dot with the arrow.

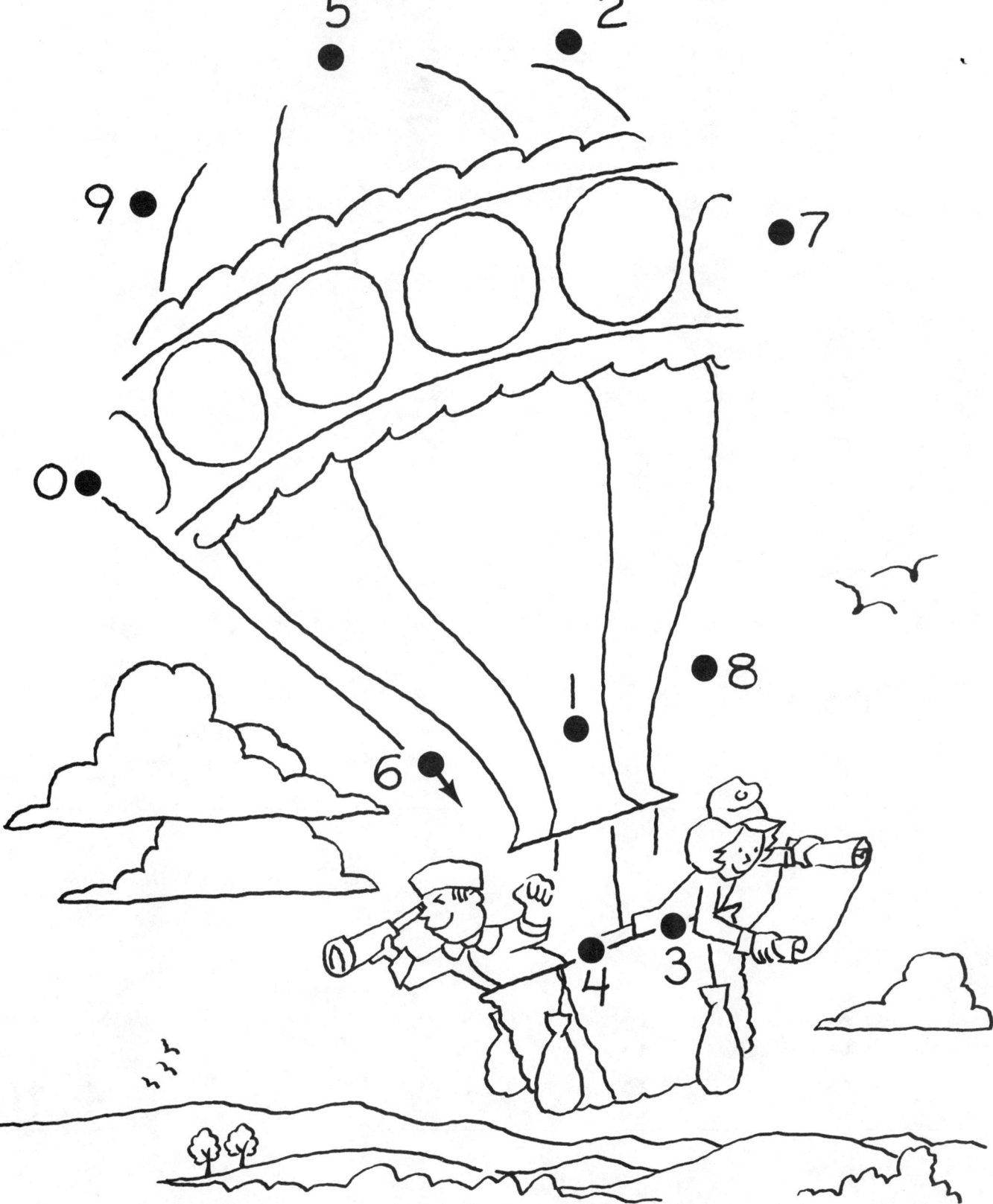

Math-A-Draw Level I

Name _____ Set 25 Worksheet **A**

Write the correct numeral on each line.

	A	B	C	D	E
1	6 + 5	3 + 5	2 + 7	8 + 5	3 + 4
2	8 + 8	10 − 5	4 + 8	10 − 9	9 + 8
3	10 − 6	8 + 7	3 + 7	10 − 4	8 − 8
4	10 − 8	6 + 8	9 + 9	10 − 7	10 + 10

Math-A-Draw Level I

Name _____   Set **25** Worksheet **B**

To find the hidden picture, draw lines from dot to dot. Follow the order of your answers. Start from the dot with the arrow.

Math-A-Draw Level I

Name _____ Set **26** Worksheet **A**

Write the correct numeral on each line.

	A	B	C	D	E
1	12 + 6	10 + 3	7 + 7	10 − 5	6 + 4
2	3 + 6	12 + 3	11 + 5	10 − 2	10 − 4
3	7 + 4	12 + 5	10 − 6	13 + 6	10 − 7
4	8 + 4	10 − 8	10 + 10	10 − 3	10 − 9

Math-A-Draw Level I

Name _____ Set **26** Worksheet **B**

To find the hidden picture, draw lines from dot to dot. Follow the order of your answers. Start from the dot with the arrow.

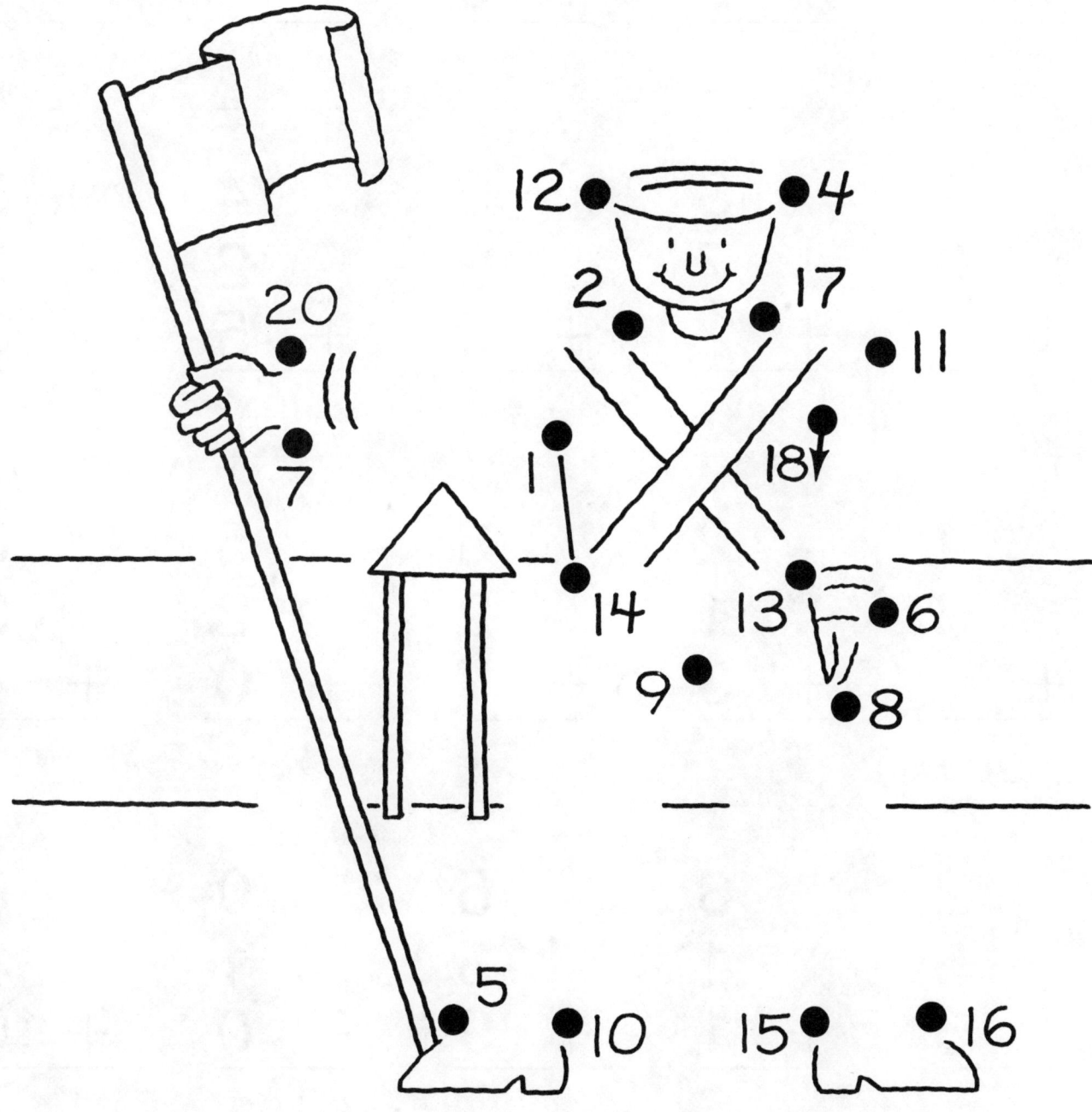

Math-A-Draw Level I

Name _____ Set **27** Worksheet **A**

Write the correct numeral on each line.

	A	B	C	D	E
1 ▶	4 5 + 7	1 1 + 2	3 6 + 9	0 2 + 1	6 3 + 8
2 ▶	1 0 + 1	3 7 + 2	2 3 + 3	4 2 + 5	3 3 + 3
3 ▶	4 3 + 7	2 1 + 3	6 2 + 7	5 2 + 0	3 3 + 4
4 ▶	2 5 + 6	3 1 + 1	5 5 + 9	0 1 + 0	6 4 + 10

Math-A-Draw Level I

Name _____ Set **27** Worksheet **B**

To find the hidden picture, draw lines from dot to dot. Follow the order of your answers. Start from the dot with the arrow.

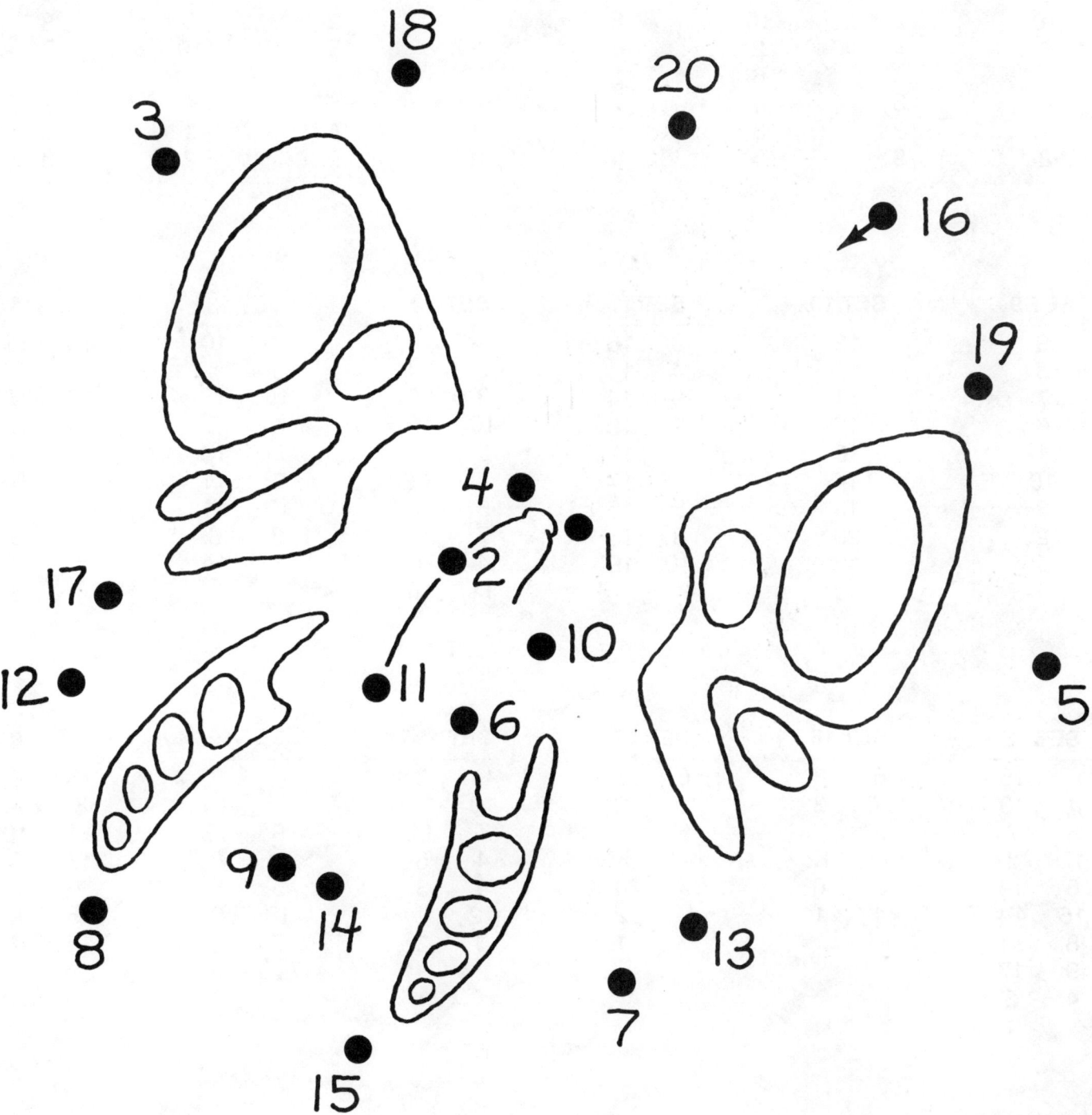

Math-A-Draw Level I

Answer Key

SET 1	SET 2	SET 3	SET 4	SET 5	SET 6	SET 7	SET 8
5	1	9	3	9	0	5	0
4	5	1	10	6	3	3	8
7	7	7	5	3	1	8	1
3	10	4	1	8	4	1	4
10	2	10	8	5	2	6	9
8	4	2	6	2	7	10	7
1	6	6	2	7	8	7	5
6	8	8	7	4	6	4	2
9	3	3	9	1	5	9	6
2	9	5	4	10	9	2	3

SET 9	SET 10	SET 11	SET 12	SET 13	SET 14
9	12	6 16	9 18	19 10	10 11
8	17	4 11	6 14	8 7	4 3
7	11	9 14	3 12	15 16	16 12
6	15	7 18	10 19	4 2	9 6
1	18	2 12	2 15	9 13	13 17
10	14	8 17	8 13	12 11	18 20
3	16	5 15	5 20	17 18	7 14
2	20	3 13	7 17	5 6	15 8
5	13	10 19	4 1	3 14	5 19
4	19		11 16		

SET 15	SET 16	SET 17	SET 18	SET 19	SET 20
18 16	5 8	6 3	14 8	10 9	16 6
10 13	10 3	11 9	10 13	14 15	8 14
5 7	2 7	5 7	7 11	6 12	11 10
12 3	11 12	10 13	4 5	11 8	13 3
6 19	9 6	4 8	9 3	5 4	7 5
15 14	4 1	12 2	12 1	13 2	15 2
8 11		1	6 2	7 3	12 4
9 17					9
4 2					
1					

Math-A-Draw Level I

SET 21		SET 22		SET 23		SET 24
15	16	11	17	16	14	6
10	8	14	12	12	9	4
14	12	10	4	15	8	1
11	3	18	2	18	4	3
7	6	8	7	10	7	8
13	4	15	6	19	3	7
17	2	13	3	17	6	2
9	5	16	5	11	2	5
		9	1	13	5	9
						0

SET 25

	A	B	C	D	E
1.	11	8	9	13	7
2.	16	5	12	1	17
3.	4	15	10	6	0
4.	2	14	18	3	20

SET 26

	A	B	C	D	E
1.	18	13	14	5	10
2.	9	15	16	8	6
3.	11	17	4	19	3
4.	12	2	20	7	1

SET 27

	A	B	C	D	E
1.	16	4	18	3	17
2.	2	12	8	11	9
3.	14	6	15	7	10
4.	13	5	19	1	20

Math-A-Draw Level I

THIS IS

_____

MATH•A•DRAW RECORD.

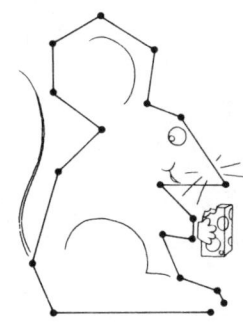

① ② ③ ④ ⑤ ⑥ ⑦ ⑧ ⑨ ⑩ ⑪ ⑫ ⑬ ⑭ ⑮ ⑯ ⑰ ⑱ ⑲ ⑳ ㉑ ㉒ ㉓ ㉔ ㉕ ㉖ ㉗

Congratulations

_____

**for excellence in
MATH•A•DRAW**

_____
TEACHER

_____
DATE

Math-A-Draw Level I

Math·A·Draw

Level II · Addition and Subtraction for Grades 1–3

27 dot-to-dot math learning games sequenced according to level of difficulty

Contents

Addition of one-digit and two-digit numerals. No regrouping   Set **1**

Subtraction of one-digit numerals from two-digit numerals. No regrouping.   Set **2**

Mixed addition and subtraction of one-digit and two-digit numerals. No regrouping.   Set **3**

Addition of two-digit numerals with zero. No regrouping.   Set **4**

Subtraction of two-digit numerals with zero. No regrouping.   Set **5**

Mixed addition and subtraction of two-digit numerals with zero. No regrouping.   Set **6**

Addition of three two-digit numerals. No regrouping.   Set **7**

Addition of two-digit numerals. No regrouping.   Set **8**

Subtraction of two-digit numerals. No regrouping.   Sets **9** and **10**

Mixed subtraction and addition of two-digit numerals. No regrouping.   Sets **11–13**

Addition of three two-digit numerals. No regrouping.   Set **14**

Addition of one-, two-, and three-digit numerals. No regrouping.   Sets **15** and **16**

Subtraction of one- and two-digit numerals from three-digit numerals. No regrouping.   Set **17**

Math-A-Draw Level II

Subtraction of two- and three-digit numerals from three-digit numerals. No regrouping.   Set **18**

Addition of three two- and three-digit numerals. No regrouping.   Set **19**

Addition of two-digit numerals. Regrouping in ten's place.   Sets **20–22**

Addition of one- and two-digit numerals. Regrouping in one's place.   Sets **23** and **24**

Addition of two-digit numerals. Regrouping in one's place.   Sets **25** and **26**

Addition of three one- and two-digit numerals. Regrouping in one's place.   Set **27**

Answer Key

Record Card and Certificate

Math-A-Draw Level II

Name _____   Set **1** Worksheet **A**

Write the correct numeral on each line.

	A	B	C	D	E
1	52 + 7	84 + 3	41 + 8	54 + 3	32 + 4
2	45 + 3	86 + 2	35 + 4	11 + 8	33 + 5
3	70 + 5	20 + 6	52 + 6	22 + 7	76 + 2
4	83 + 6	72 + 7	41 + 3	92 + 3	83 + 3

Math-A-Draw Level II

Name _____ Set **1** Worksheet **B**

To find the hidden picture, draw lines from dot to dot. Follow the order of your answers. Start from the dot with the arrow.

Math-A-Draw Level II

Name _____   Set **2** Worksheet **A**

Write the correct numeral on each line.

	A	B	C	D	E
1	95 − 5	67 − 7	69 − 8	53 − 1	57 − 4
2	79 − 2	88 − 2	66 − 3	89 − 7	86 − 3
3	49 − 8	77 − 4	39 − 4	46 − 6	57 − 3
4	23 − 1	34 − 2	78 − 6	38 − 7	87 − 6

Math-A-Draw Level II

Name _____ Set **2** Worksheet **B**

To find the hidden picture, draw lines from dot to dot. Follow the order of your answers. Start from the dot with the arrow.

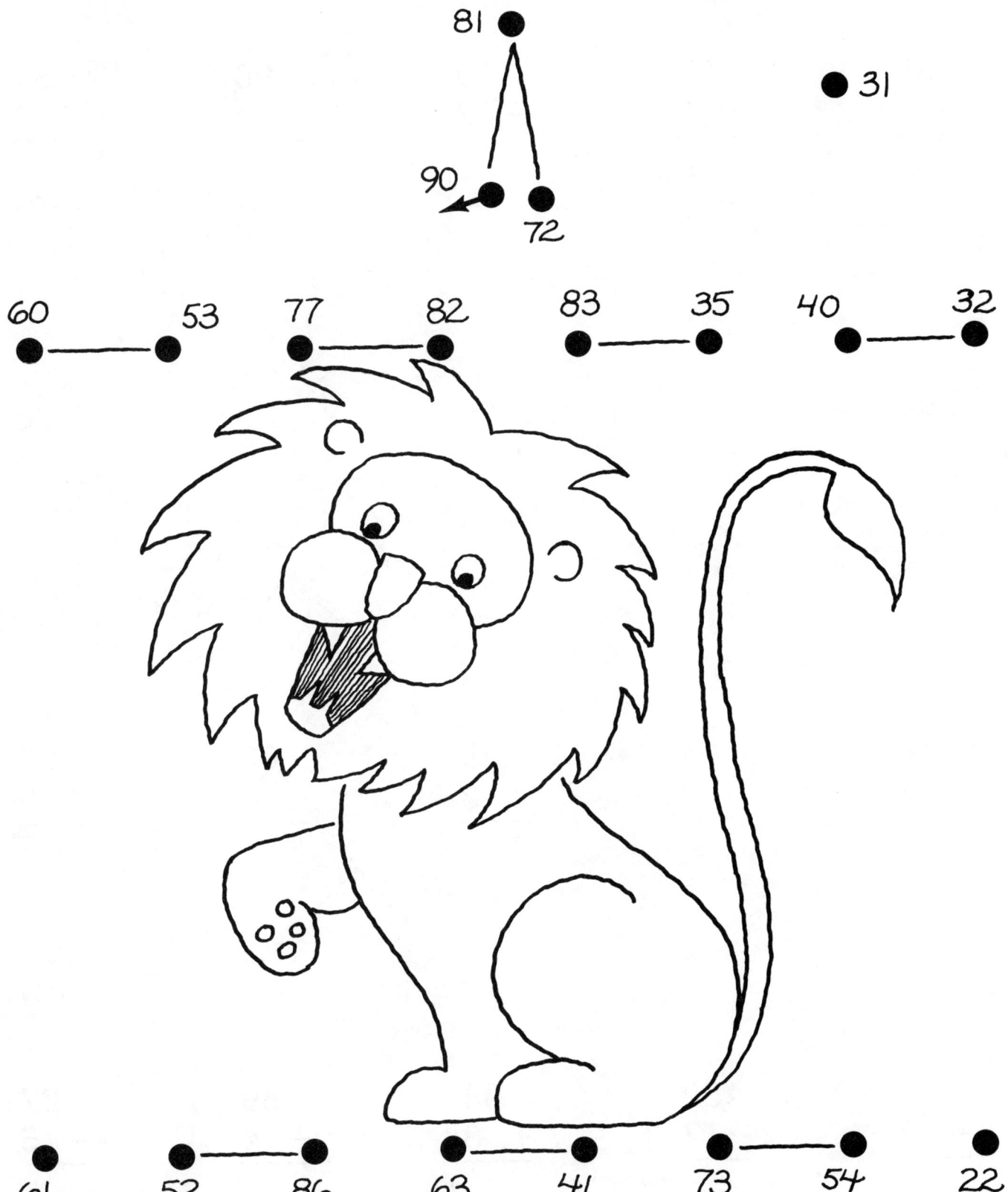

Math-A-Draw Level II

Name _____ Set **3** Worksheet **A**

Write the correct numeral on each line.

	A	B	C	D	E
1	88 − 2	34 + 5	79 − 2	90 + 4	86 − 3
2	95 + 3	38 − 7	29 − 8	85 + 4	76 + 2
3	44 − 2	94 + 2	28 − 3	63 + 4	19 − 8
4	17 + 2	59 − 7	94 + 3	89 − 4	27 − 5

Math-A-Draw Level II

Name _____ Set **3** Worksheet **B**

To find the hidden picture, draw lines from dot to dot. Follow the order of your answers. Start from the dot with the arrow.

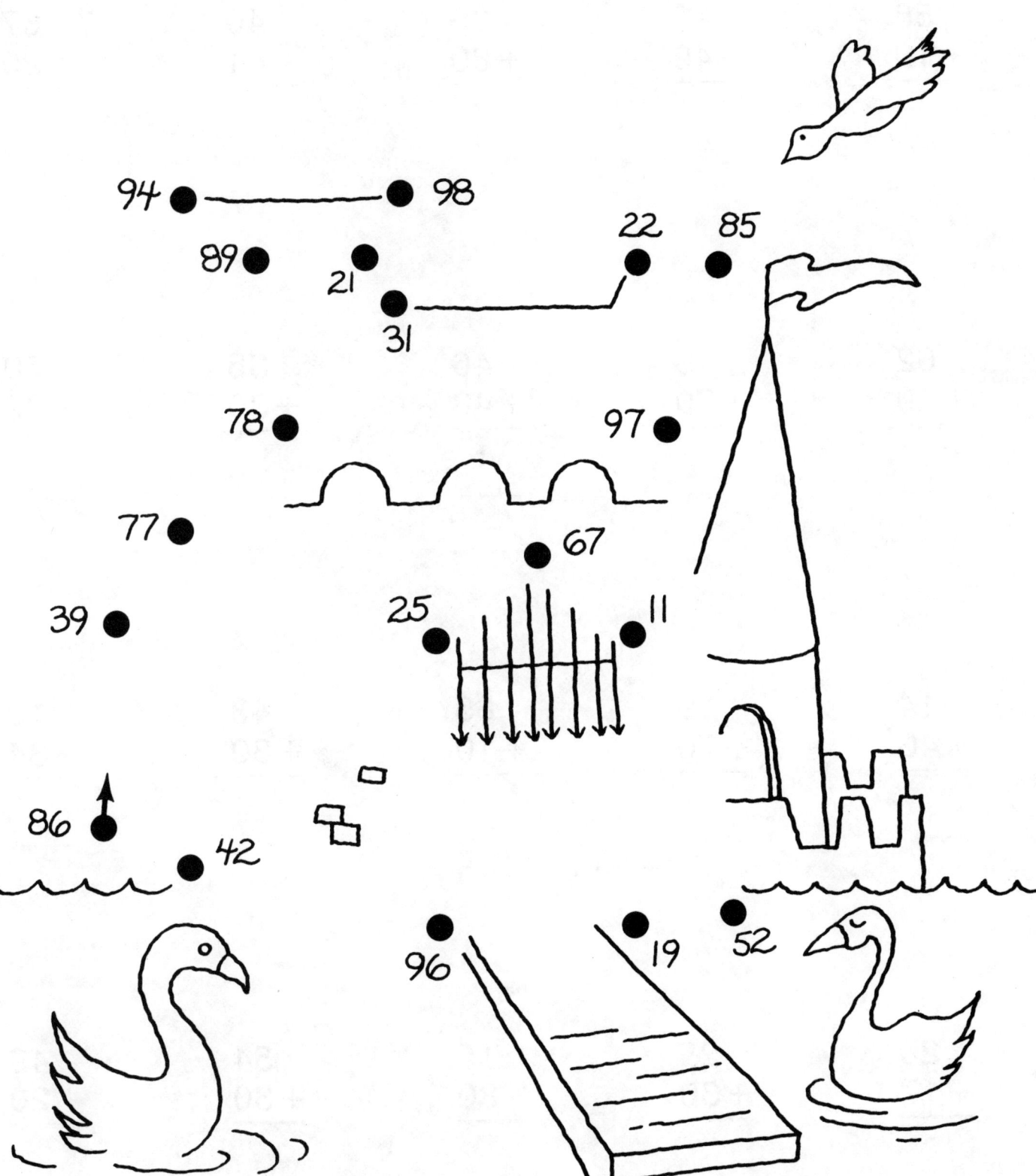

Math-A-Draw Level II

Name _____   Set **4** Worksheet **A**

Write the correct numeral on each line.

	A	B	C	D	E
1	58 +10	12 +40	39 +60	40 +41	67 +20
2	62 +20	18 +70	46 +40	35 +30	70 +22
3	14 +40	19 +70	65 +10	43 +30	10 +34
4	20 +17	25 +30	15 +80	54 +30	49 +20

Math-A-Draw Level II

Name _____ Set **4** Worksheet **B**

To find the hidden picture, draw lines from dot to dot. Follow the order of your answers. Start from the dot with the arrow.

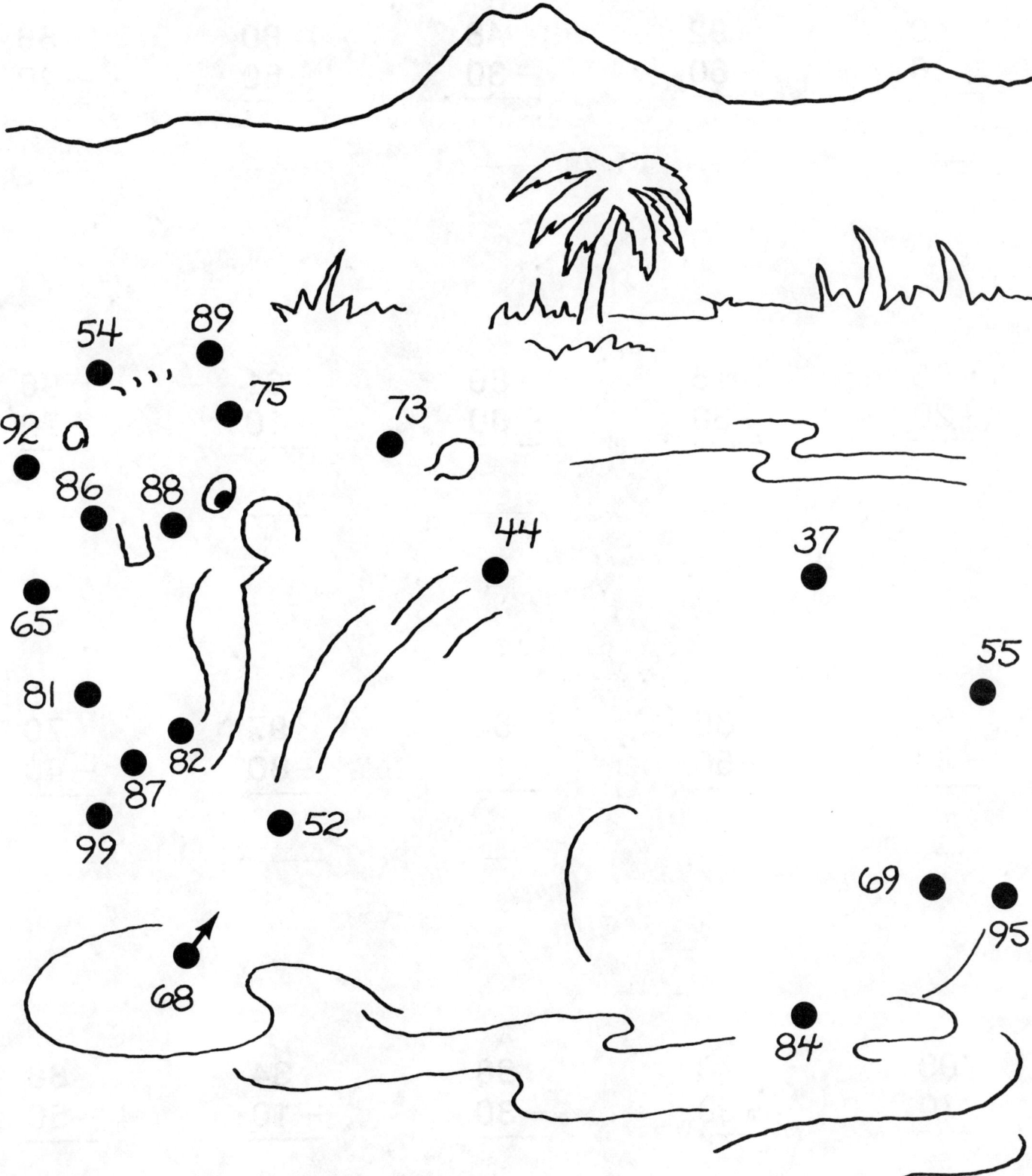

Math-A-Draw Level II

Name _____   Set 5 Worksheet **A**

Write the correct numeral on each line.

	A	B	C	D	E
1	49 −30	92 −60	48 −30	90 −50	56 −40
2	95 −20	55 −30	80 −60	61 −10	96 −70
3	53 −20	86 −50	54 −10	97 −80	70 −40
4	93 −70	78 −50	88 −30	34 −10	88 −50

Math-A-Draw Level II

Name _____ Set 5 Worksheet B

To find the hidden picture, draw lines from dot to dot. Follow the order of your answers. Start from the dot with the arrow.

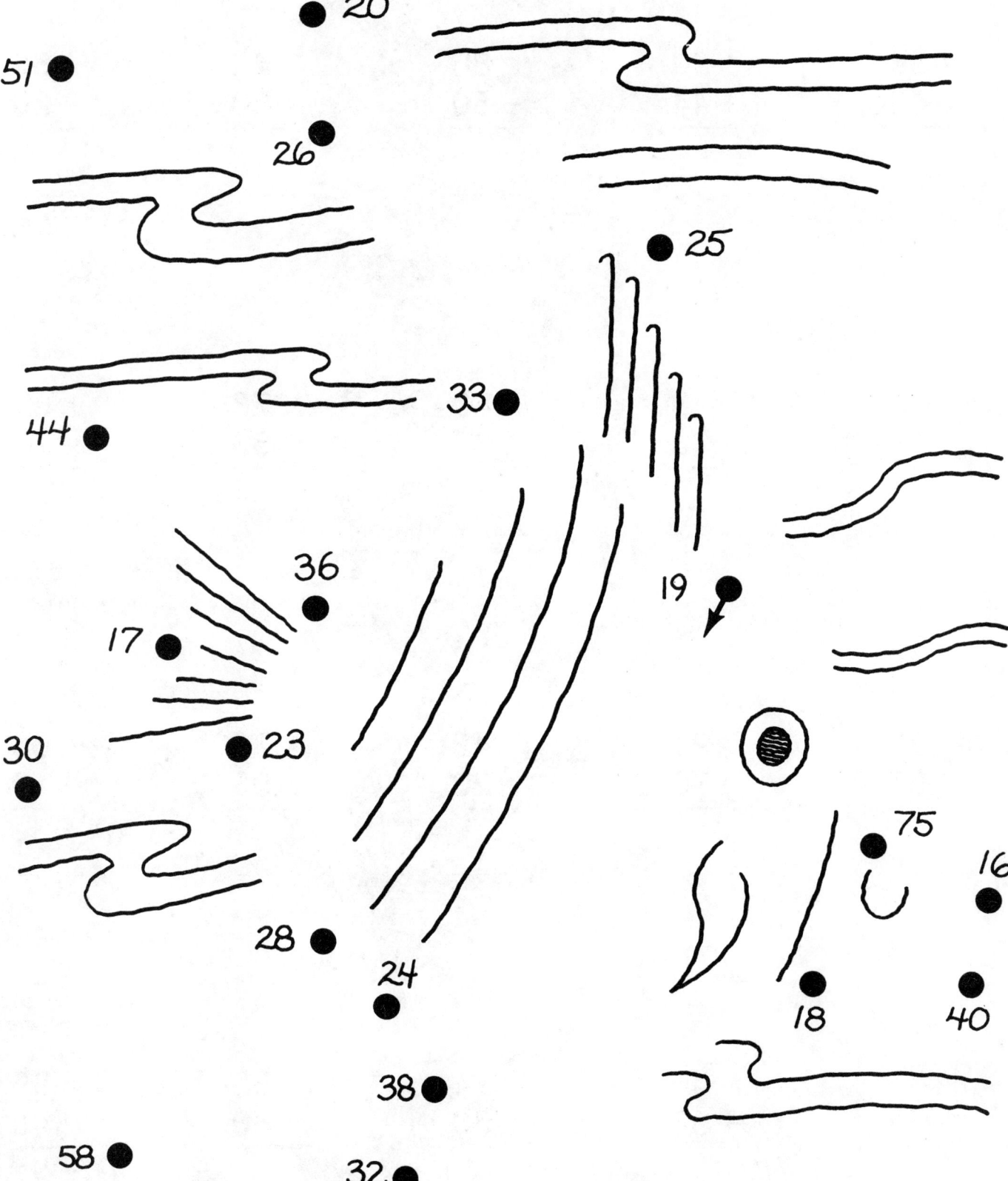

Math-A-Draw Level II

Name _____   Set **6** Worksheet **A**

Write the correct numeral on each line.

	A	B	C	D	E
1	96 − 40	20 + 44	86 − 50	42 + 50	80 − 30
2	20 + 79	48 − 30	60 + 37	73 − 50	97 − 70
3	30 + 65	91 − 70	42 + 20	78 − 50	86 + 10
4	83 − 50	30 + 57	74 − 30	35 + 50	86 − 40

Math-A-Draw Level II

Name _____   Set **6** Worksheet **B**

To find the hidden picture, draw lines from dot to dot. Follow the order of your answers. Start from the dot with the arrow.

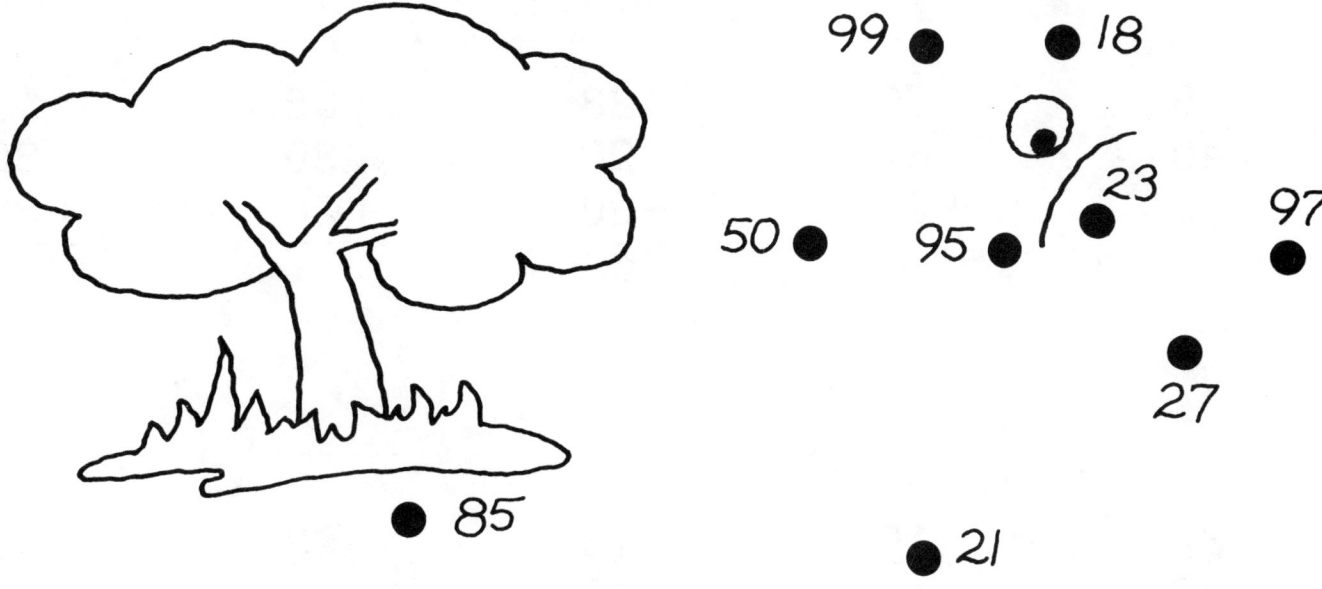

Math-A-Draw Level II

Name _____ Set **7** Worksheet **A**

Write the correct numeral on each line.

	A	B	C	D	E
1	20 40 +32 ――	30 30 +27 ――	23 20 +30 ――	36 30 +20 ――	15 30 +50 ――
2	34 40 +10 ――	29 40 +30 ――	18 40 +30 ――	23 30 +40 ――	50 19 +20 ――
3	20 31 +30 ――	20 10 +35 ――	20 20 +14 ――	10 18 +40 ――	50 13 +20 ――
4	28 10 +20 ――	20 39 +10 ――	36 30 +30 ――	10 10 +17 ――	30 25 +20 ――

Math-A-Draw Level II

Name _____ Set **7** Worksheet **B**

To find the hidden picture, draw lines from dot to dot. Follow the order of your answers. Start from the dot with the arrow.

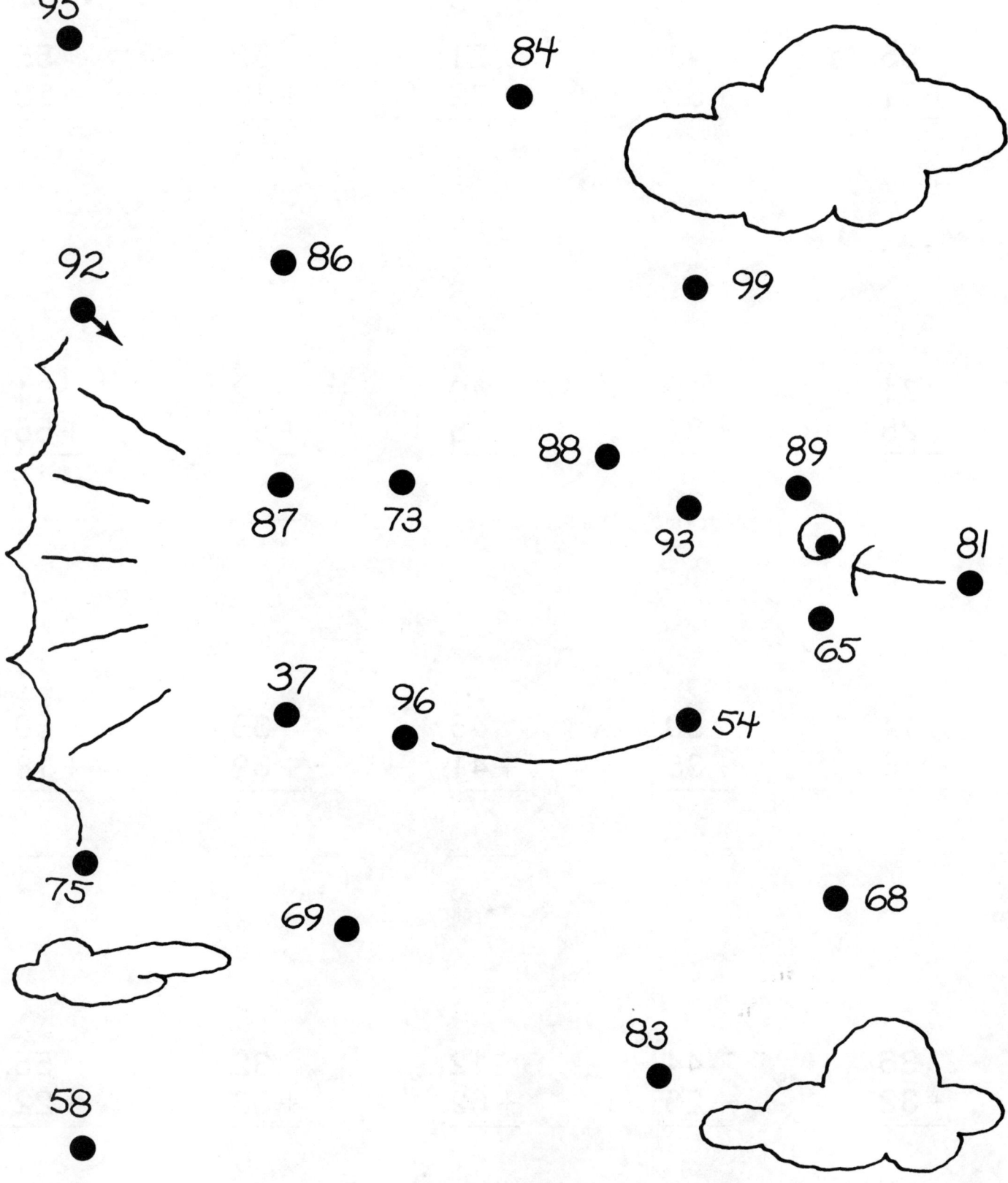

Math-A-Draw Level II

Name _____ Set **8** Worksheet **A**

Write the correct numeral on each line.

	A	B	C	D	E
1	55 +31	41 +57	21 +72	82 +15	55 +20
2	71 +28	12 +84	40 +18	12 +67	21 +55
3	11 +78	50 +38	46 +41	33 +62	60 +18
4	36 +32	44 +25	12 +82	32 +53	55 +22

Math-A-Draw Level II

Name _____   Set **8** Worksheet **B**

To find the hidden picture, draw lines from dot to dot. Follow the order of your answers. Start from the dot with the arrow.

Math-A-Draw Level II

Name _____ Set **9** Worksheet **A**

Write the correct numeral on each line.

	A	B	C	D	E
1	43 −23	86 −24	99 −13	75 −20	58 −33
2	28 −14	75 −43	58 −22	76 −23	72 −31
3	54 −32	76 −52	66 −53	42 −31	81 −30
4	56 −40	82 −51	95 −12	85 −62	74 −31

Math-A-Draw Level II

Name _____   Set **9** Worksheet **B**

To find the hidden picture, draw lines from dot to dot. Follow the order of your answers. Start from the dot with the arrow.

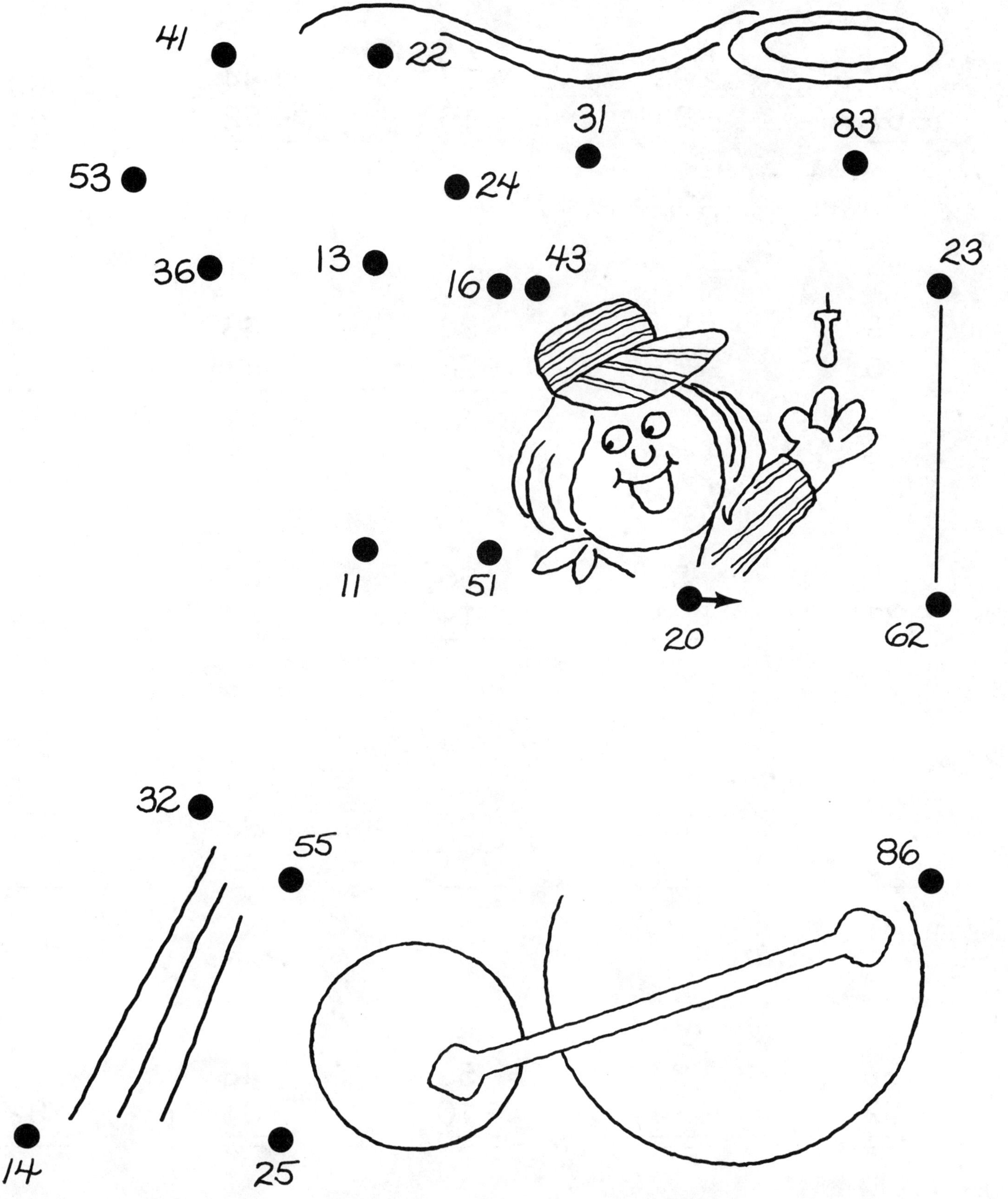

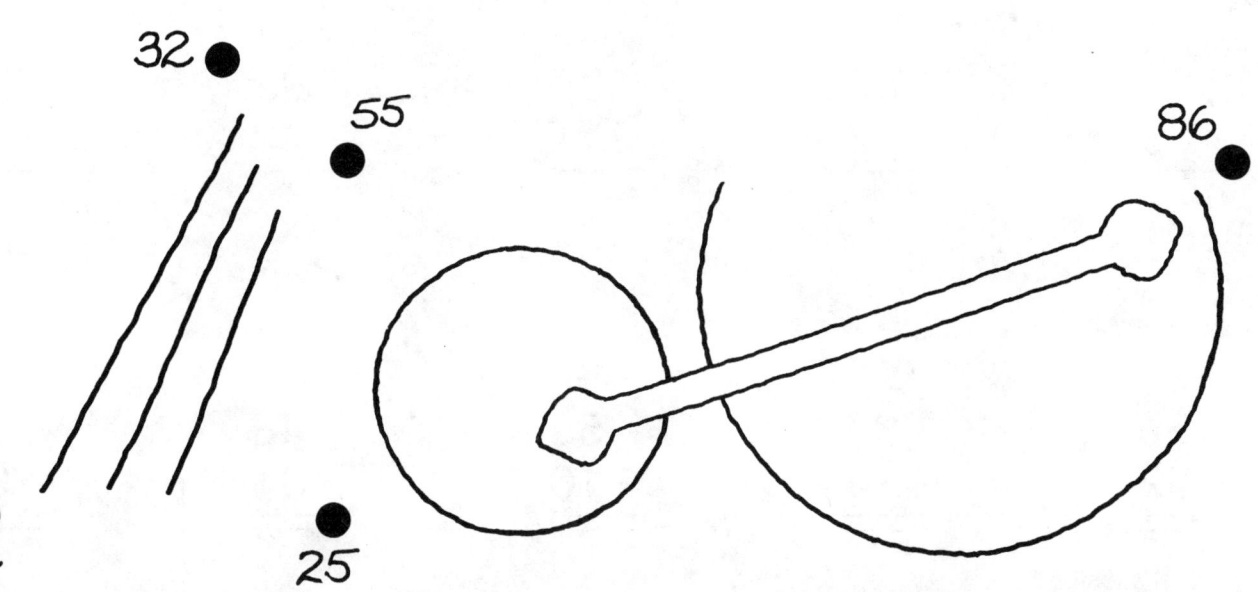

Math-A-Draw Level II

Name _____ Set **10** Worksheet **A**

Write the correct numeral on each line.

	A	B	C	D	E
1	97 −67	88 −23	77 −16	84 −52	86 −41
2	49 −25	98 −67	36 −25	63 −51	84 −61
3	95 −21	37 −24	85 −14	84 −34	79 −64
4	95 −75	69 −18	91 −11	82 −72	55 −14
5	54 −32	37 −16	58 −16	48 −31	79 −32

Math-A-Draw Level II

Name _____ Set **10** Worksheet **B**

To find the hidden picture, draw lines from dot to dot. Follow the order of your answers. Start from the dot with the arrow.

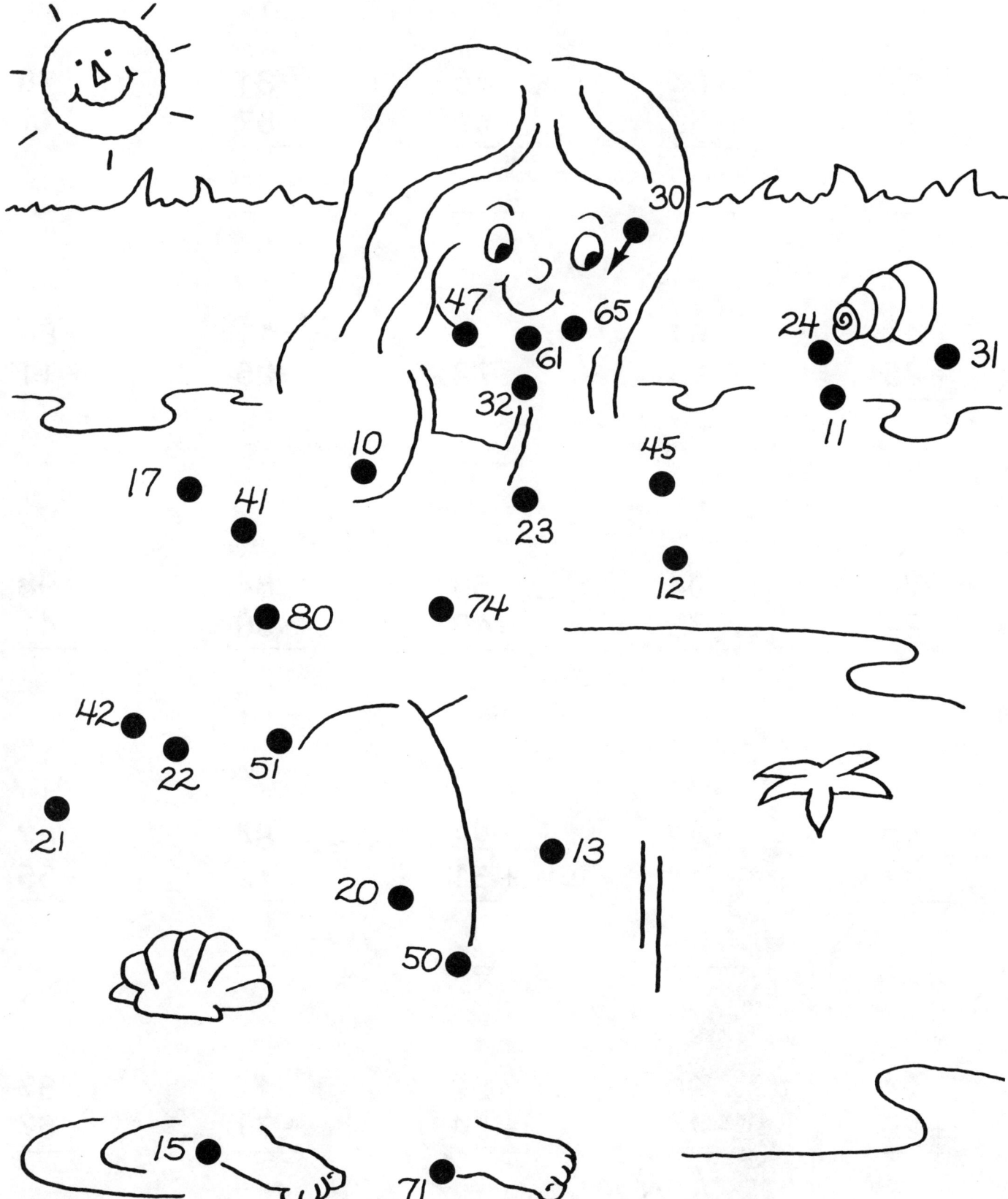

Math-A-Draw Level II

Name _____ Set **11** Worksheet **A**

Write the correct numeral on each line.

	A	B	C	D	E
1	31 +57	64 −52	40 +59	31 +67	78 −11
2	44 +25	61 +16	87 −72	11 +25	80 +11
3	76 −22	94 −32	58 −42	84 −50	98 −41
4	42 +47	48 −17	28 +51	84 +12	87 −55
5	24 +25	96 −44	22 +54	14 +71	87 −67

Math-A-Draw Level II

Name _____ Set **11** Worksheet **B**

To find the hidden picture, draw lines from dot to dot. Follow the order of your answers. Start from the dot with the arrow.

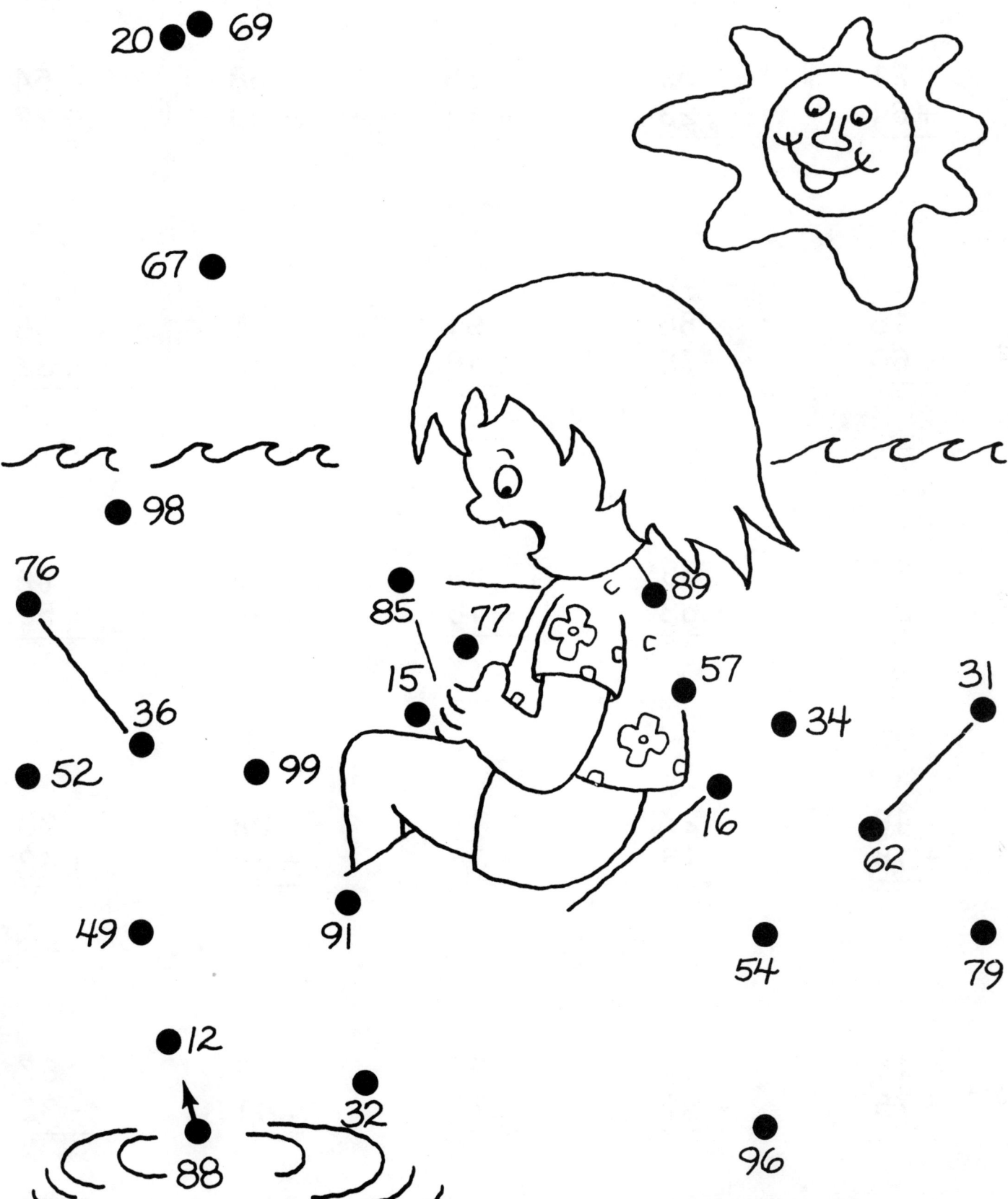

Math-A-Draw Level II

Name _____ Set 12 Worksheet A

Write the correct numeral on each line.

	A	B	C	D	E
1	21 +64	59 −23	75 +14	68 −53	54 +22
2	18 +60	88 −75	91 −40	25 +72	56 −32
3	37 −25	88 −62	59 −18	33 +51	77 −50
4	40 +18	27 −16	12 +34	22 +55	33 +42
5	11 +75	63 −41	94 −73	46 +41	67 −33

Math-A-Draw Level II

Name _____   Set **12** Worksheet **B**

To find the hidden picture, draw lines from dot to dot. Follow the order of your answers. Start from the dot with the arrow.

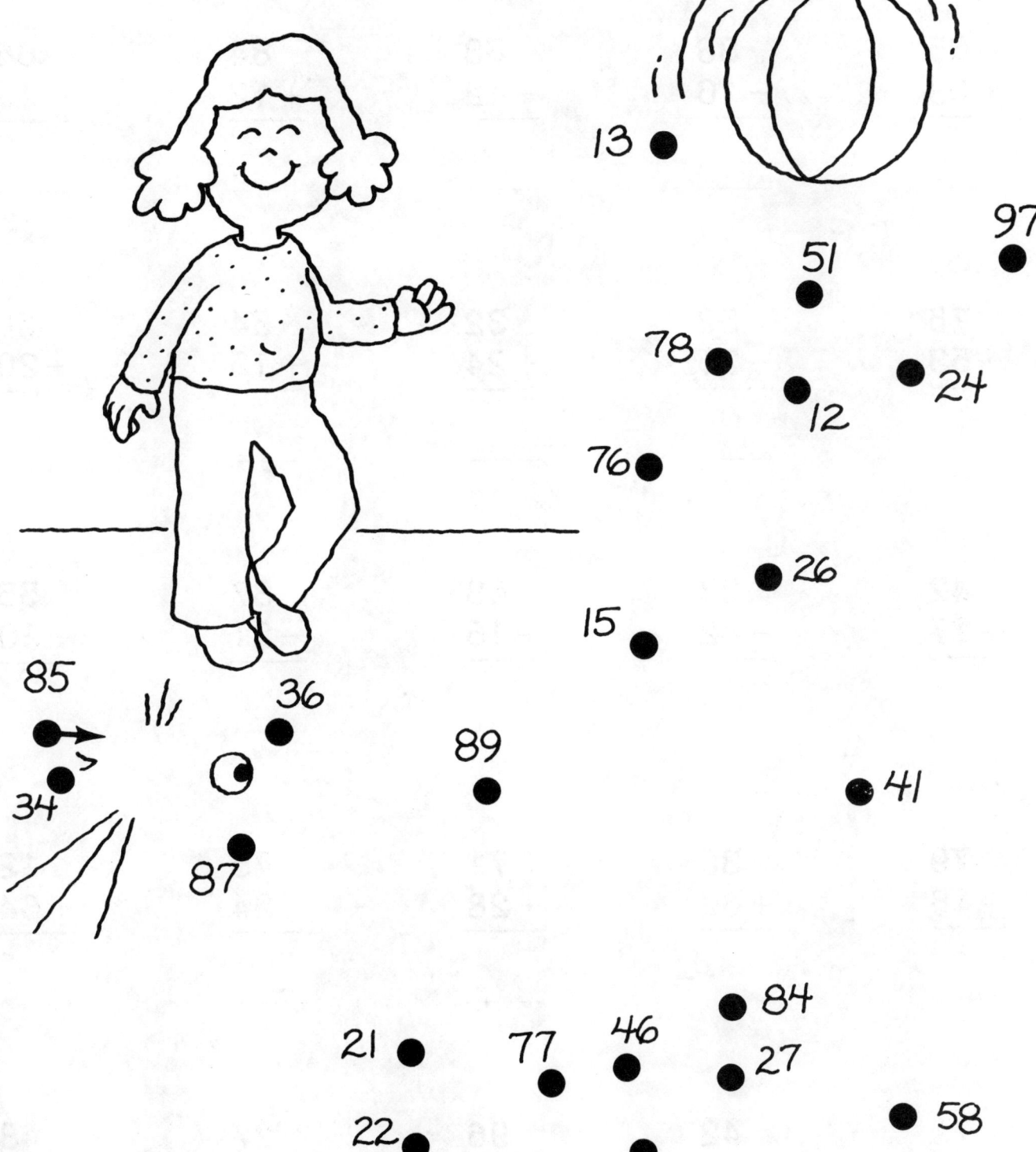

Math-A-Draw Level II

Name _____   Set **13**   Worksheet **A**

Write the correct numeral on each line.

	A	B	C	D	E
1	65 +13	86 −16	63 −12	84 +12	65 −41
2	75 −53	52 −21	32 +24	54 +15	74 −20
3	42 +17	87 −42	48 −16	87 −27	55 +13
4	79 −46	30 +62	71 +28	45 −24	12 +64
5	79 −36	42 +35	96 −33	27 +62	48 −33

Math-A-Draw Level II

Name _____ Set **13** Worksheet **B**

To find the hidden picture, draw lines from dot to dot. Follow the order of your answers. Start from the dot with the arrow.

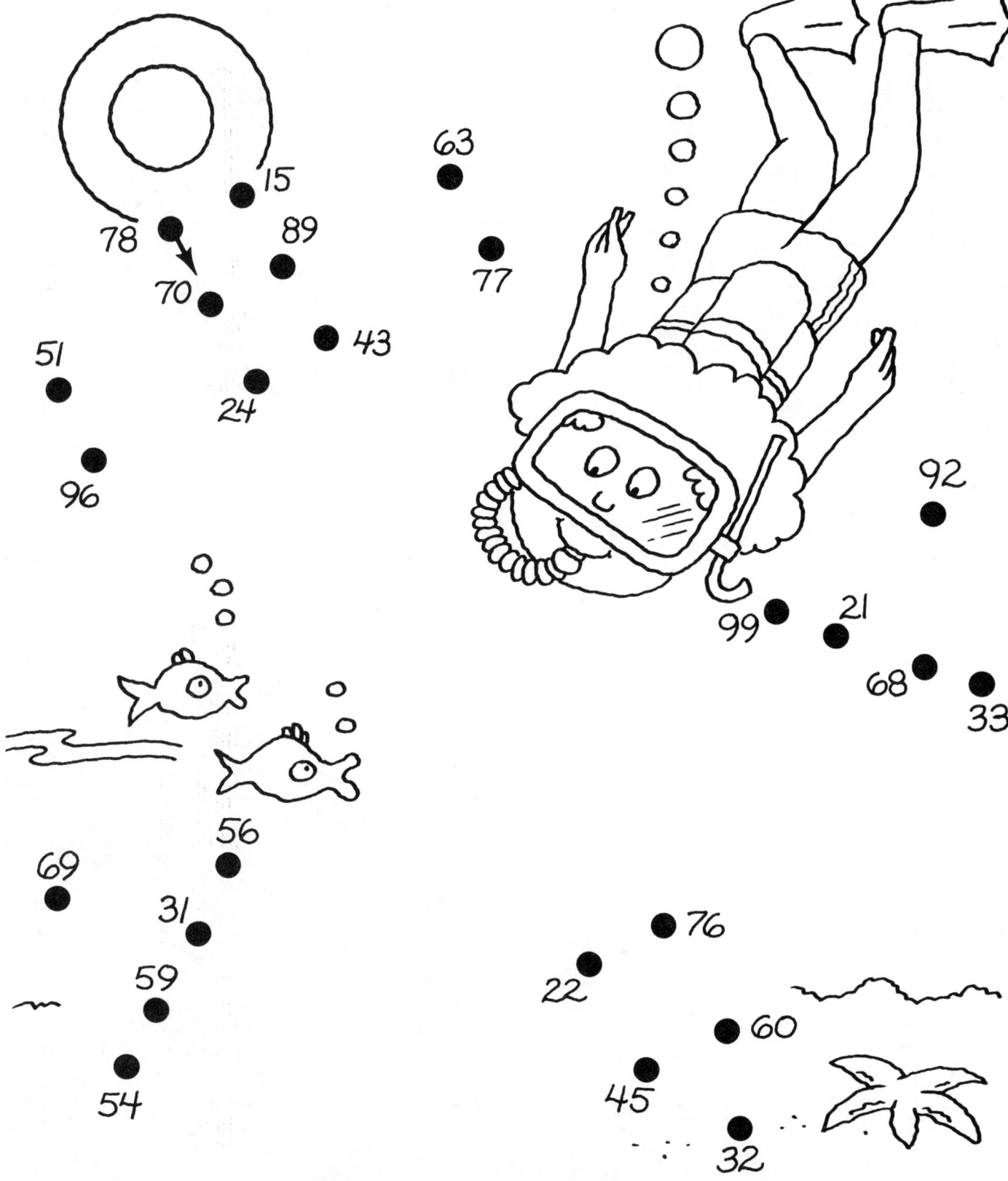

Math-A-Draw Level II

Name _____   Set **14**   Worksheet **A**

Write the correct numeral on each line.

	A	B	C	D	E
1	60 11 +21	20 32 +35	21 30 +22	30 44 +12	50 12 +33
2	42 20 +22	50 17 +32	10 23 +55	20 41 +32	14 40 +35
3	30 20 +31	21 13 +31	12 32 +10	42 13 +13	10 50 +23
4	14 22 +22	12 24 +33	32 32 +32	12 12 +13	31 32 +12

Math-A-Draw Level II

Name _____ Set **14** Worksheet **B**

To find the hidden picture, draw lines from dot to dot. Follow the order of your answers. Start from the dot with the arrow.

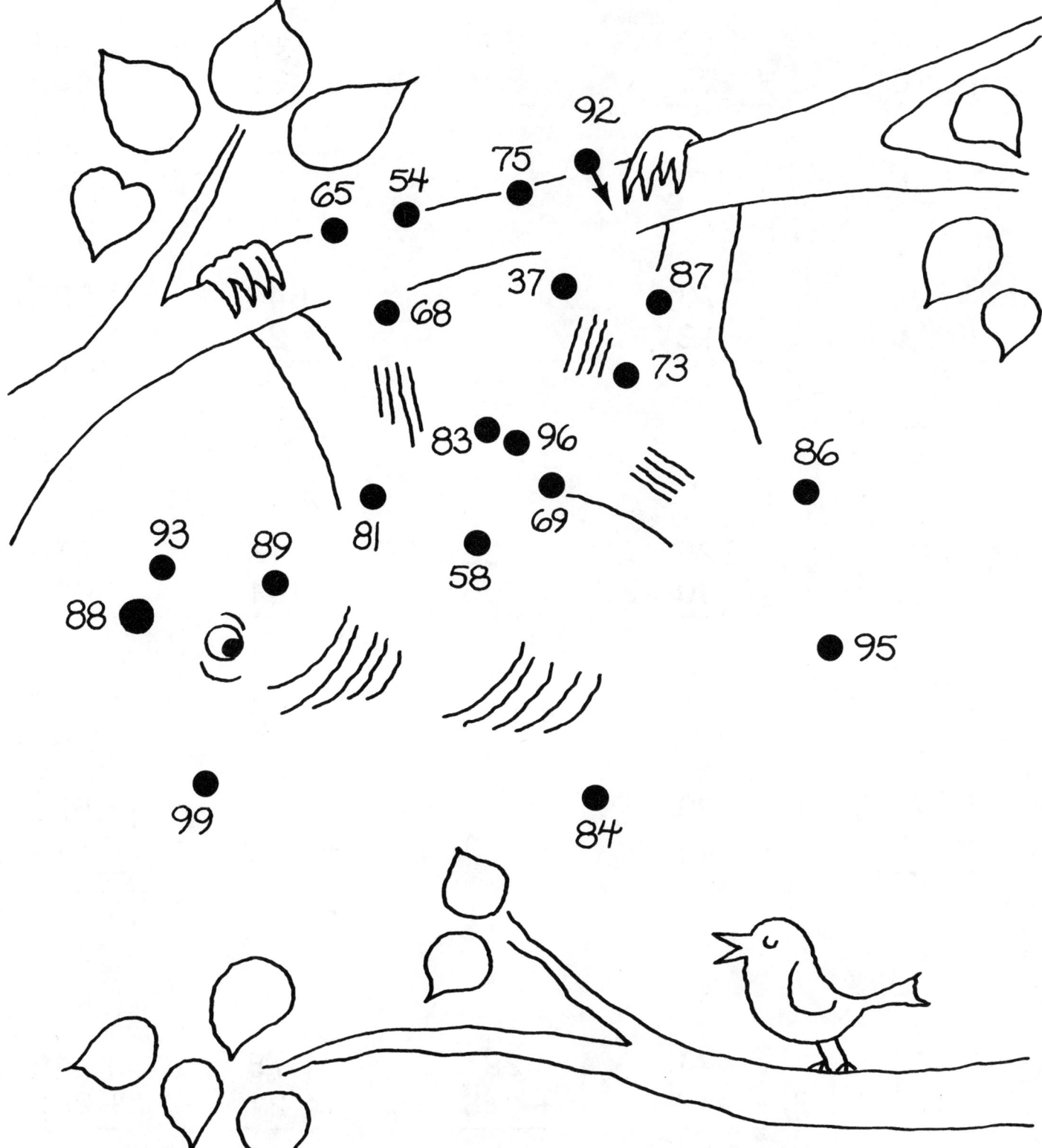

Math-A-Draw Level II

Name _____ Set **15** Worksheet **A**

Write the correct numeral on each line.

	A	B	C	D	E
1	447 + 20	360 +129	203 +514	901 + 35	104 +480
2	694 + 5	473 + 12	336 + 52	643 + 26	232 + 47
3	806 +102	320 + 40	63 +705	18 +401	250 +609
4	771 + 7	23 +842	125 + 53	53 +216	565 + 14
5	854 + 13	44 +912	291 + 8	578 + 21	46 +242

Math-A-Draw Level II

Name _____ Set **15** Worksheet **B**

To find the hidden picture, draw lines from dot to dot. Follow the order of your answers. Start from the dot with the arrow.

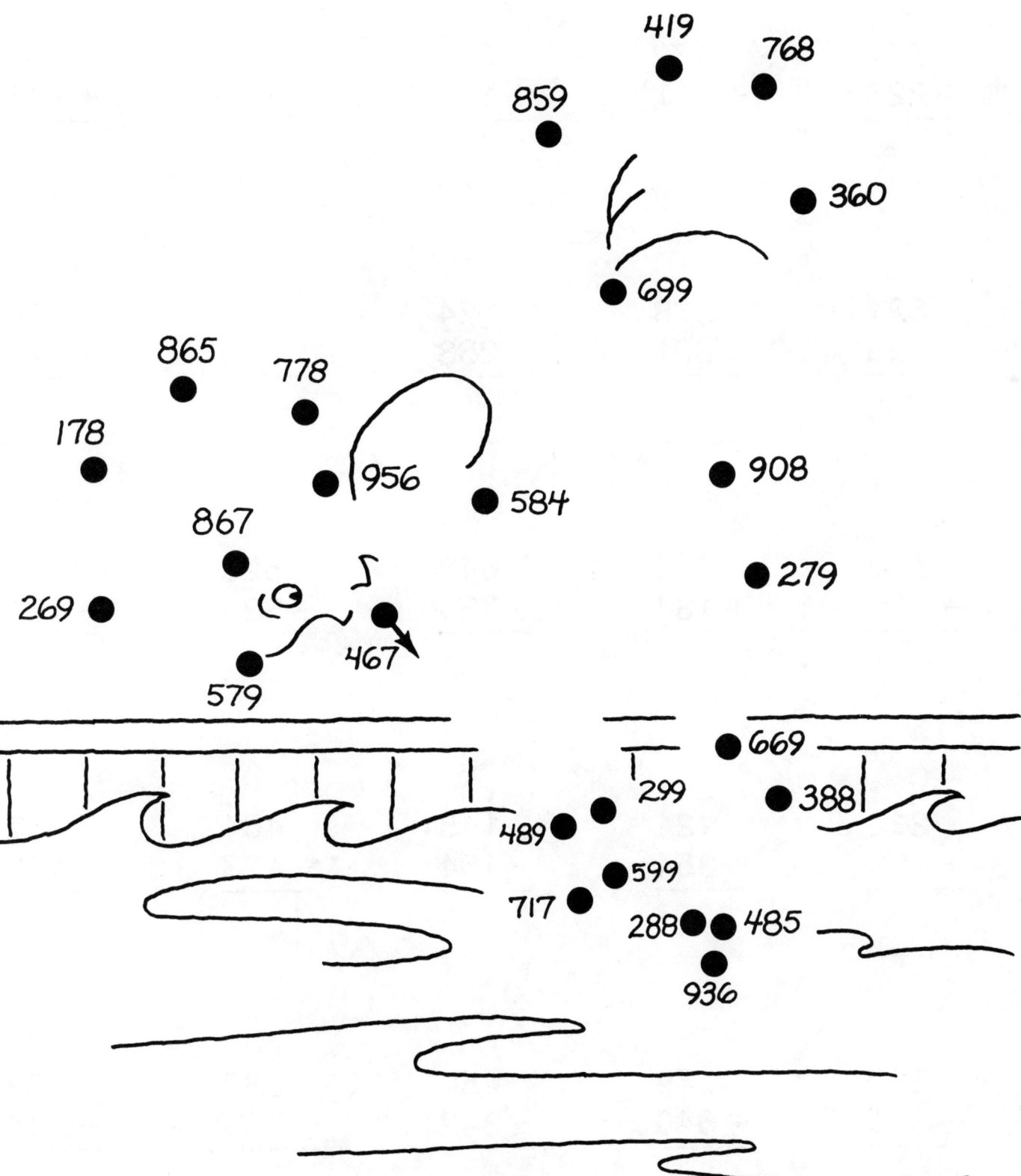

Math-A-Draw Level II

Name _____ Set **16** Worksheet **A**

Write the correct numeral on each line.

	A	B	C	D	E
1	764 +223	432 +517	765 +123	157 +741	32 +946
2	621 +326	278 +621	124 +253	33 +156	465 + 22
3	520 +406	724 +134	642 +323	523 +324	331 +364
4	212 +465	121 +854	145 +154	464 +423	57 +432
5	212 +520	49 +640	454 +342	232 +354	652 +344

Math-A-Draw Level II

Name _____ Set **16** Worksheet **B**

To find the hidden picture, draw lines from dot to dot. Follow the order of your answers. Start from the dot with the arrow.

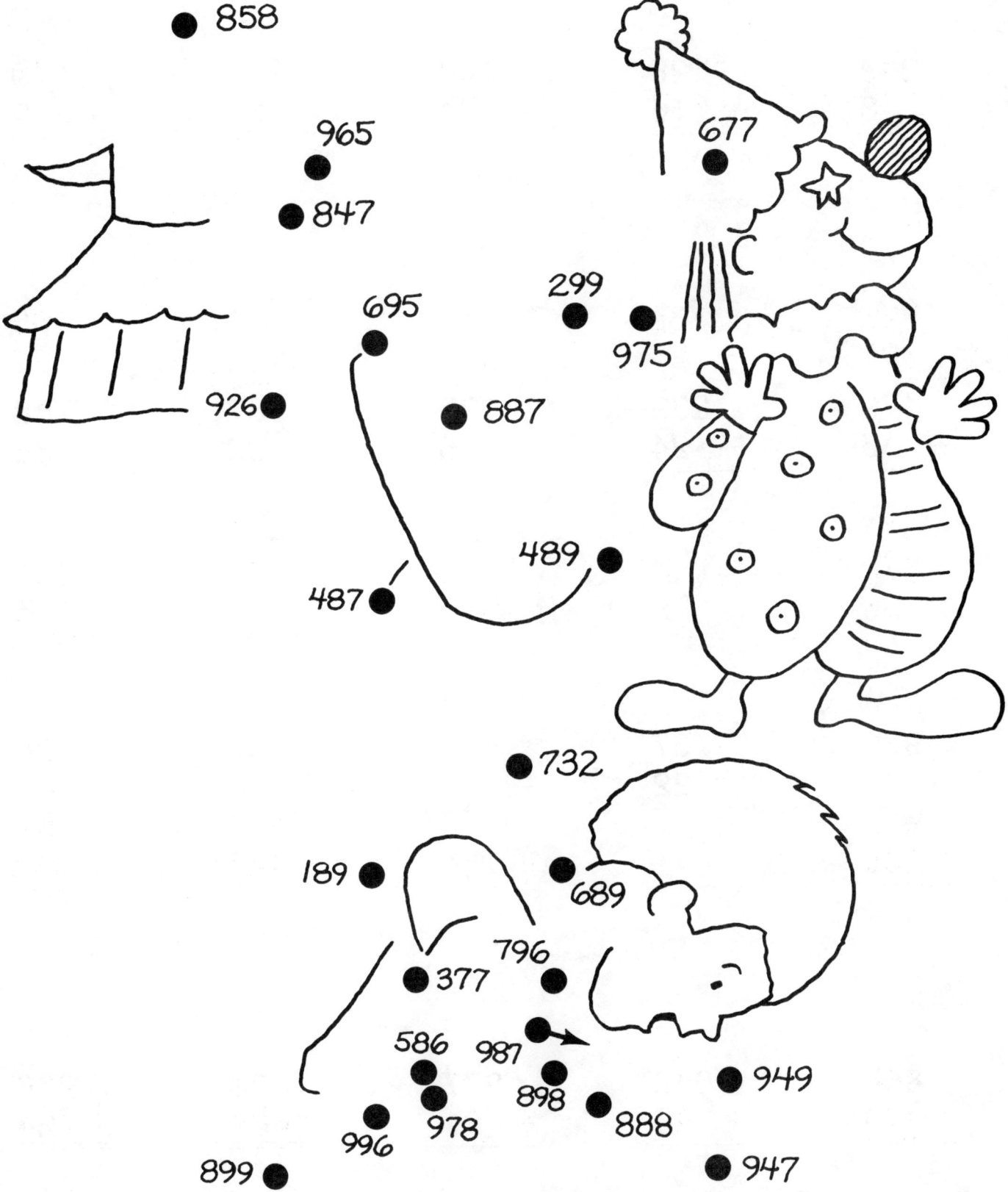

Math-A-Draw Level II

Name _____ Set **17** Worksheet **A**

Write the correct numeral on each line.

	A	B	C	D	E
1	219 − 18	128 − 16	187 − 64	748 − 34	479 − 2
2	479 − 5	239 − 24	198 − 56	187 − 63	748 − 35
3	989 − 41	757 − 22	559 − 47	387 − 4	796 − 45
4	865 − 13	648 − 3	877 − 21	498 − 67	266 − 24

Math-A-Draw Level II

Name _____   Set **17** Worksheet **B**

To find the hidden picture, draw lines from dot to dot. Follow the order of your answers. Start from the dot with the arrow.

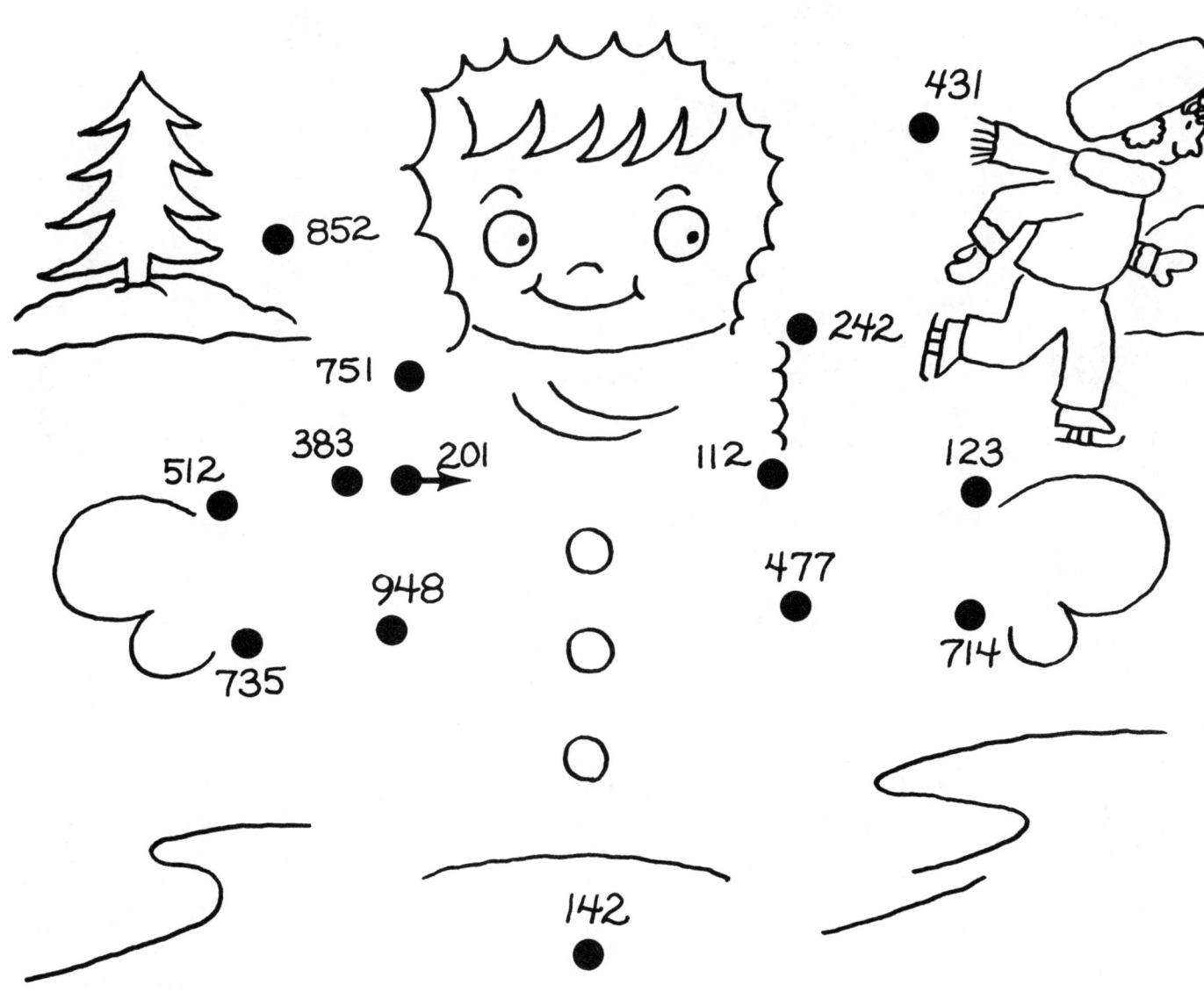

Math-A-Draw Level II

Name _____   Set **18** Worksheet **A**

Write the correct numeral on each line.

	A	B	C	D	E
1	930 − 910	547 − 241	498 − 363	188 − 65	905 − 705
2	793 − 262	165 − 31	898 − 731	667 − 265	793 − 453
3	886 − 342	689 − 581	767 − 732	794 − 744	846 − 221
4	579 − 550	377 − 47	909 − 208	238 − 124	654 − 432

Math-A-Draw Level II

Name _____   Set **18** Worksheet **B**

To find the hidden picture, draw lines from dot to dot. Follow the order of your answers. Start from the dot with the arrow.

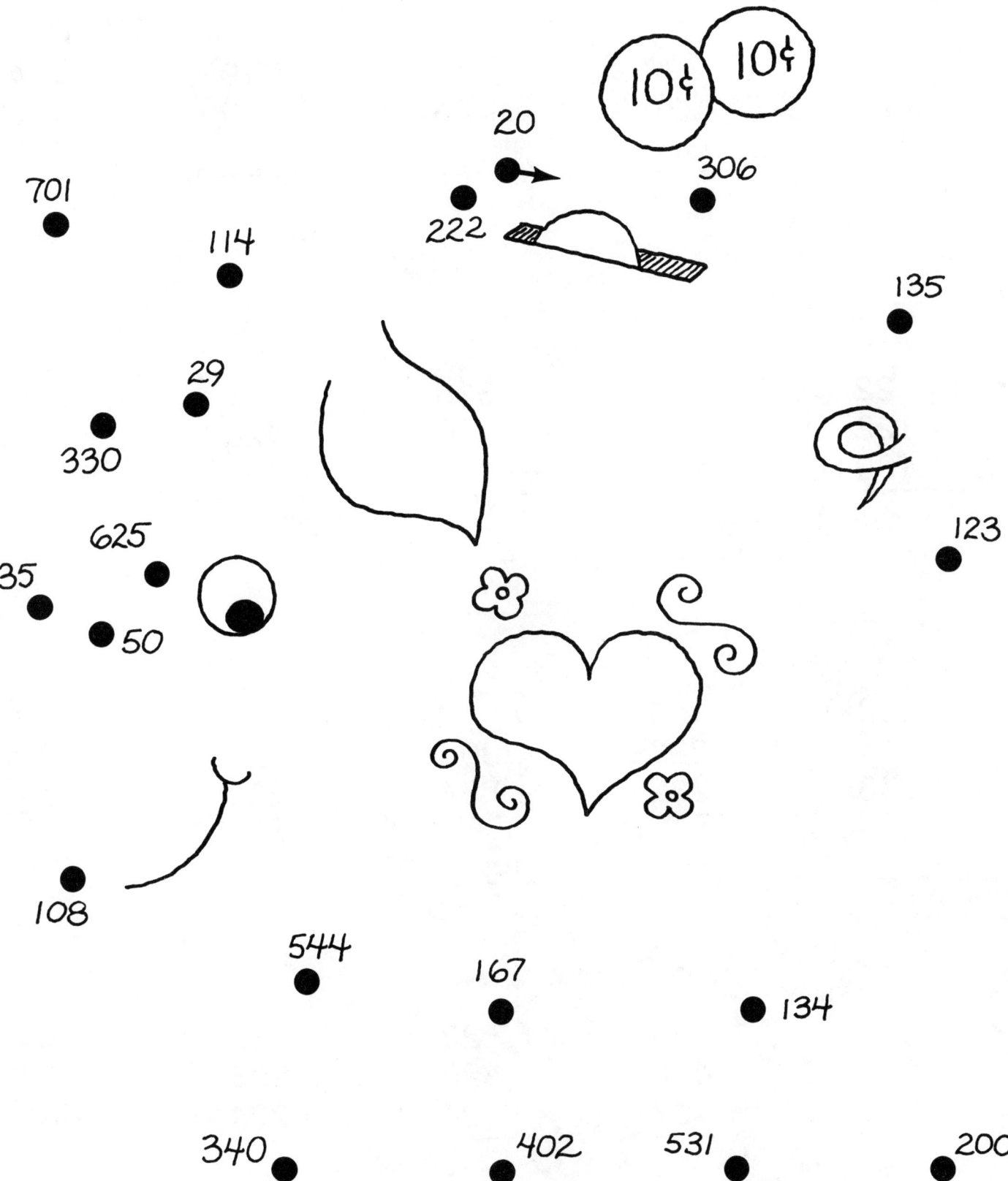

Math-A-Draw Level II

Name _____   Set **19**   Worksheet **A**

Write the correct numeral on each line.

	A	B	C	D	E
1	212 443 + 123	322 220 + 323	912 23 + 21	710 125 + 32	14 610 + 312
2	22 122 + 135	303 212 + 202	315 210 + 334	23 423 + 203	320 35 + 344
3	202 44 + 243	115 232 + 232	2 302 + 604	321 222 + 225	312 120 + 152
4	320 220 + 45	35 430 + 134	23 320 + 124	10 205 + 204	21 22 + 345

Math-A-Draw Level II

Name _____ Set **19** Worksheet **B**

To find the hidden picture, draw lines from dot to dot. Follow the order of your answers. Start from the dot with the arrow.

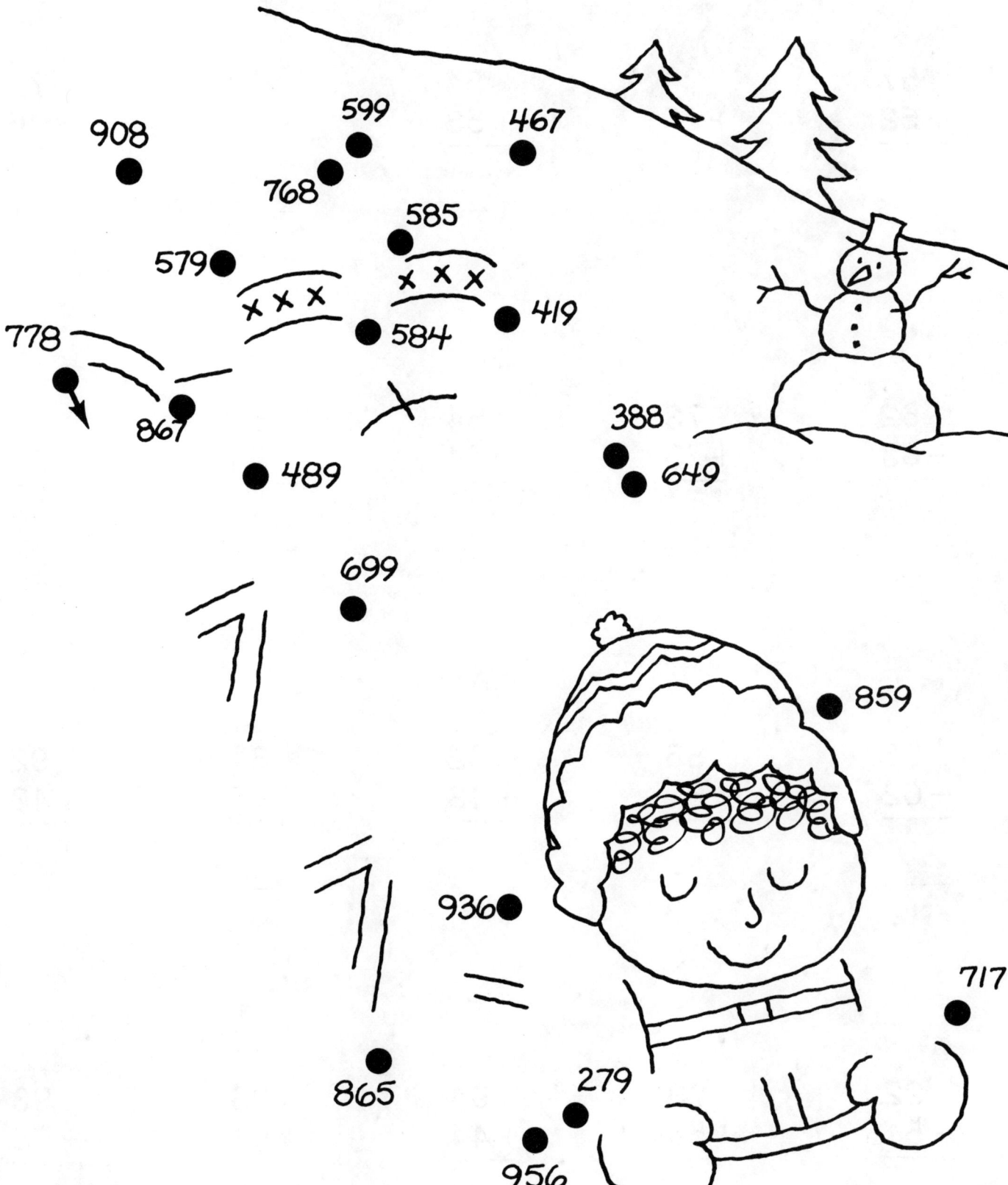

Math-A-Draw Level II

Name _____ Set **20** Worksheet **A**

Write the correct numeral on each line.

	A	B	C	D	E
1	57 +52	34 +25	54 +53	78 +41	72 +36
2	62 +63	73 +73	54 +44	52 +64	72 +32
3	95 +62	86 +81	62 +43	81 +41	92 +43
4	92 +51	73 +54	94 +44	93 +84	93 +75

Math-A-Draw Level II

Name _____ Set **20** Worksheet **B**

To find the hidden picture, draw lines from dot to dot. Follow the order of your answers. Start from the dot with the arrow.

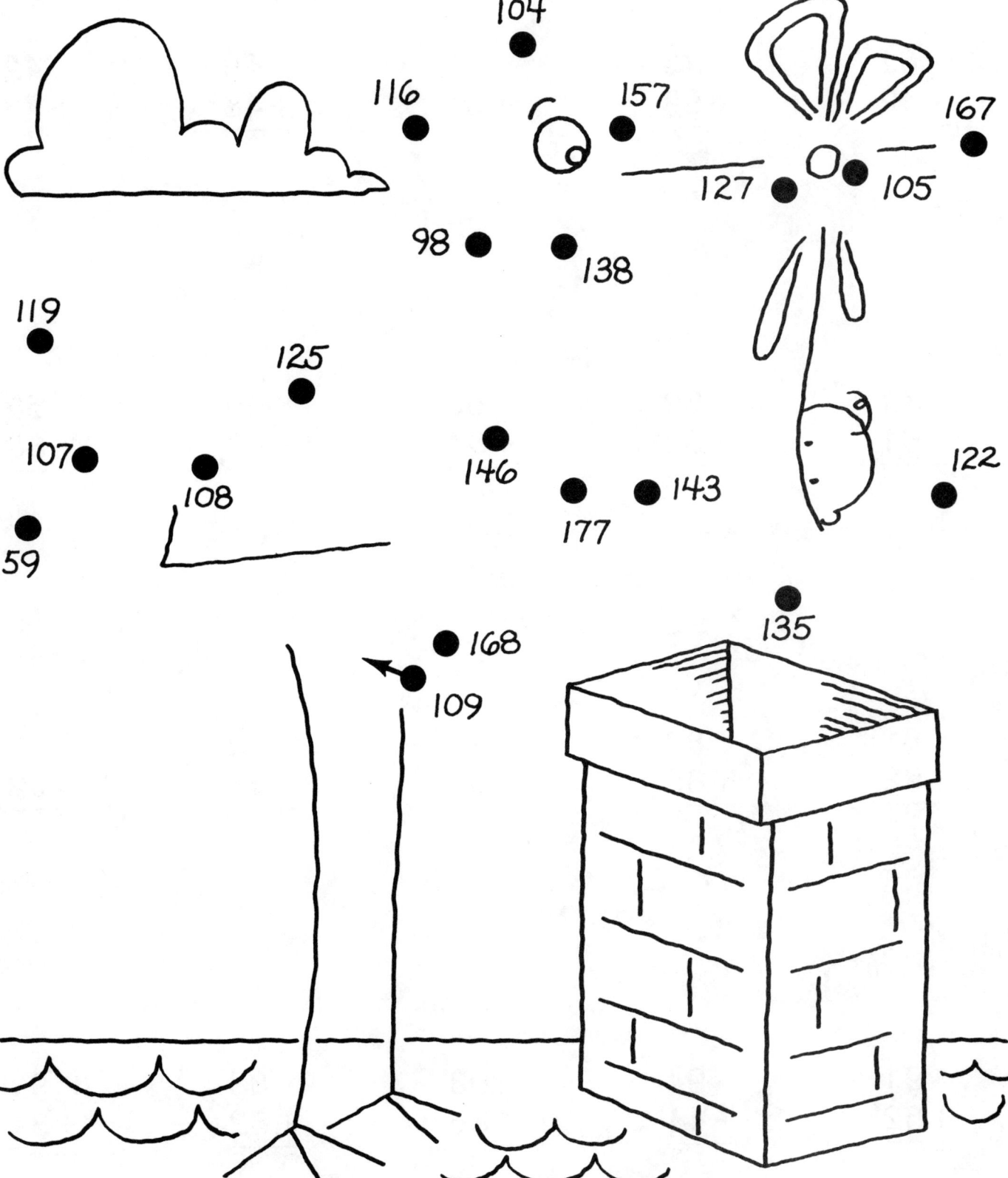

Math-A-Draw Level II

Name _____ Set **21** Worksheet **A**

Write the correct numeral on each line.

	A	B	C	D	E
1	61 +42	73 +53	65 +63	60 +48	42 +73
2	74 +61	62 +52	55 +54	60 +60	63 +83
3	61 +92	83 +85	93 +84	72 +67	96 +62
4	91 +52	94 +44	93 +36	83 +82	91 +81

Math-A-Draw Level II

Name _____ Set **21** Worksheet **B**

To find the hidden picture, draw lines from dot to dot. Follow the order of your answers. Start from the dot with the arrow.

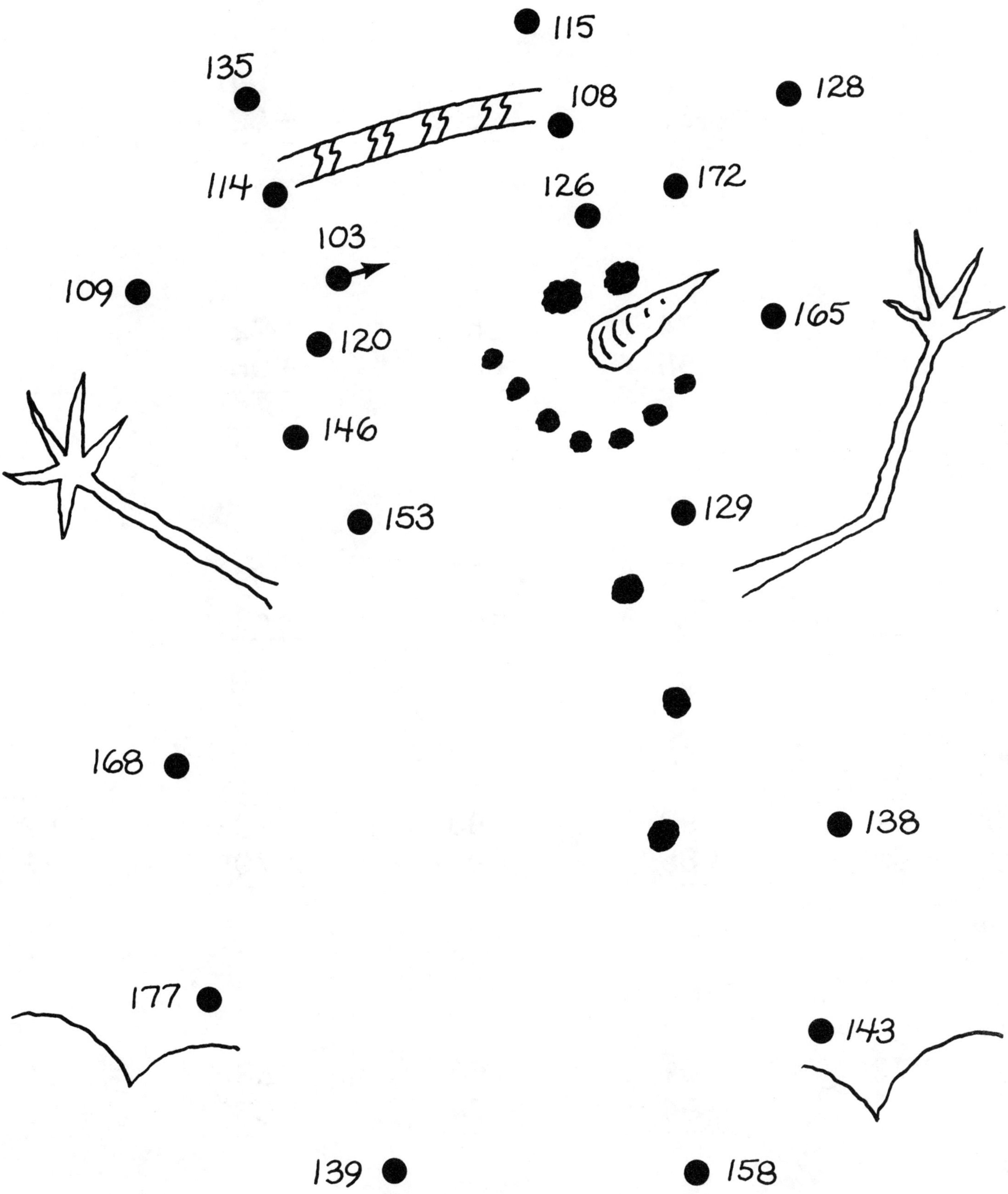

• 115

135 •
• 108   • 128

114 •
126 •   • 172

• 103 →

109 •
• 120   • 165

• 146

• 153   • 129

168 •
                                    • 138

177 •
                                         • 143

139 •   • 158

Math-A-Draw Level II

Name _____ Set **22** Worksheet **A**

Write the correct numeral on each line.

	A	B	C	D	E
1	92 +64	72 +67	62 +63	94 +52	75 +63
2	63 +86	74 +55	51 +81	72 +95	83 +90
3	63 +95	92 +72	85 +83	94 +84	94 +32
4	91 +52	83 +65	83 +94	93 +70	62 +73
5	72 +73	61 +94	53 +74	83 +85	83 +96

Math-A-Draw Level II

Name _____ Set **22** Worksheet **B**

To find the hidden picture, draw lines from dot to dot. Follow the order of your answers. Start from the dot with the arrow.

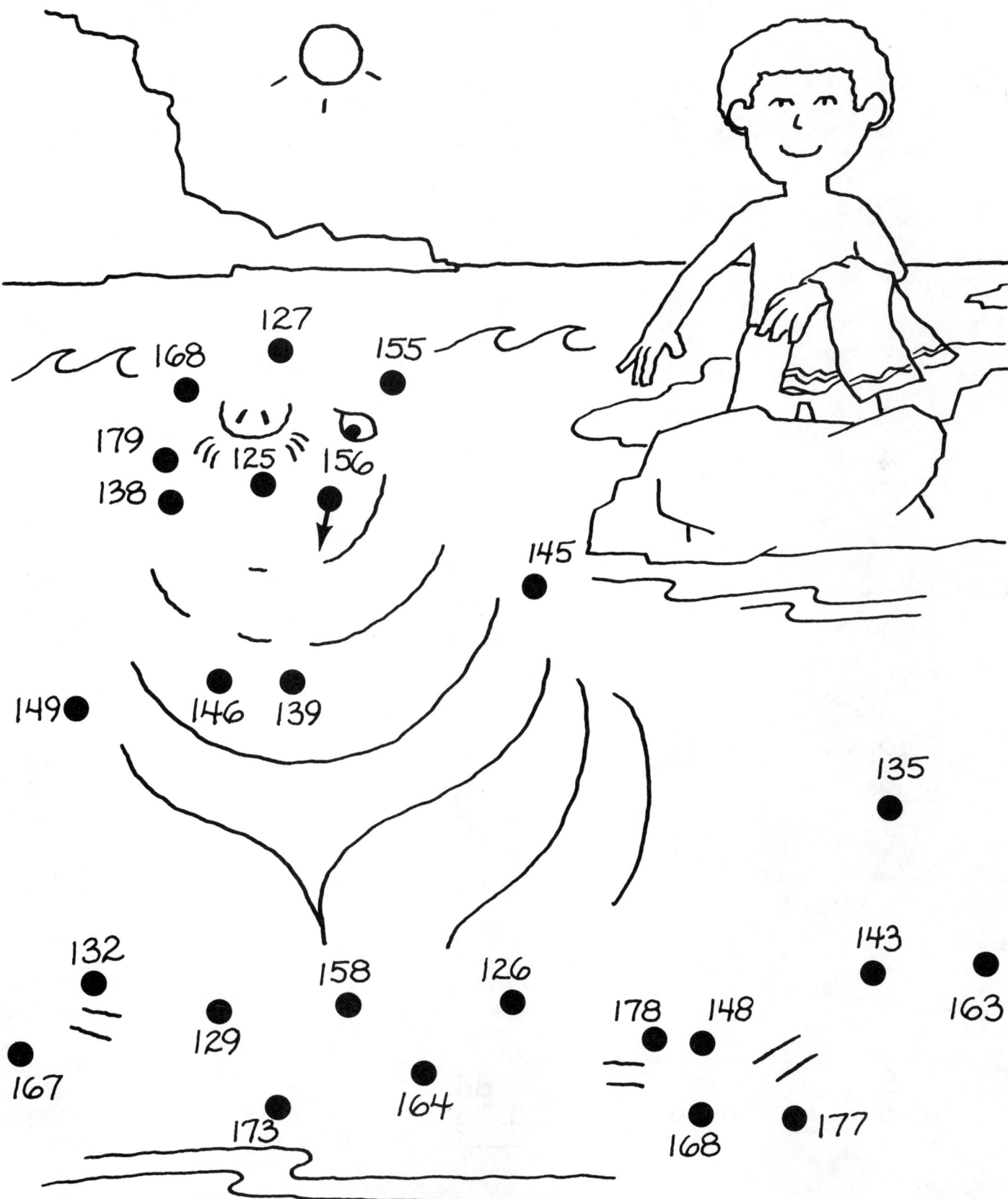

Math-A-Draw Level II

Name _____ Set **23** Worksheet **A**

Write the correct numeral on each line.

	A	B	C	D	E
1	52 + 8	48 + 6	53 + 9	38 + 5	65 + 7
2	69 + 4	18 + 9	64 + 7	56 + 8	85 + 7
3	42 + 9	83 + 8	74 + 8	36 + 9	39 + 3
4	26 + 9	47 + 3	84 + 9	31 + 9	28 + 4

Math-A-Draw Level II

Name _____ Set **23** Worksheet **B**

To find the hidden picture, draw lines from dot to dot. Follow the order of your answers. Start from the dot with the arrow.

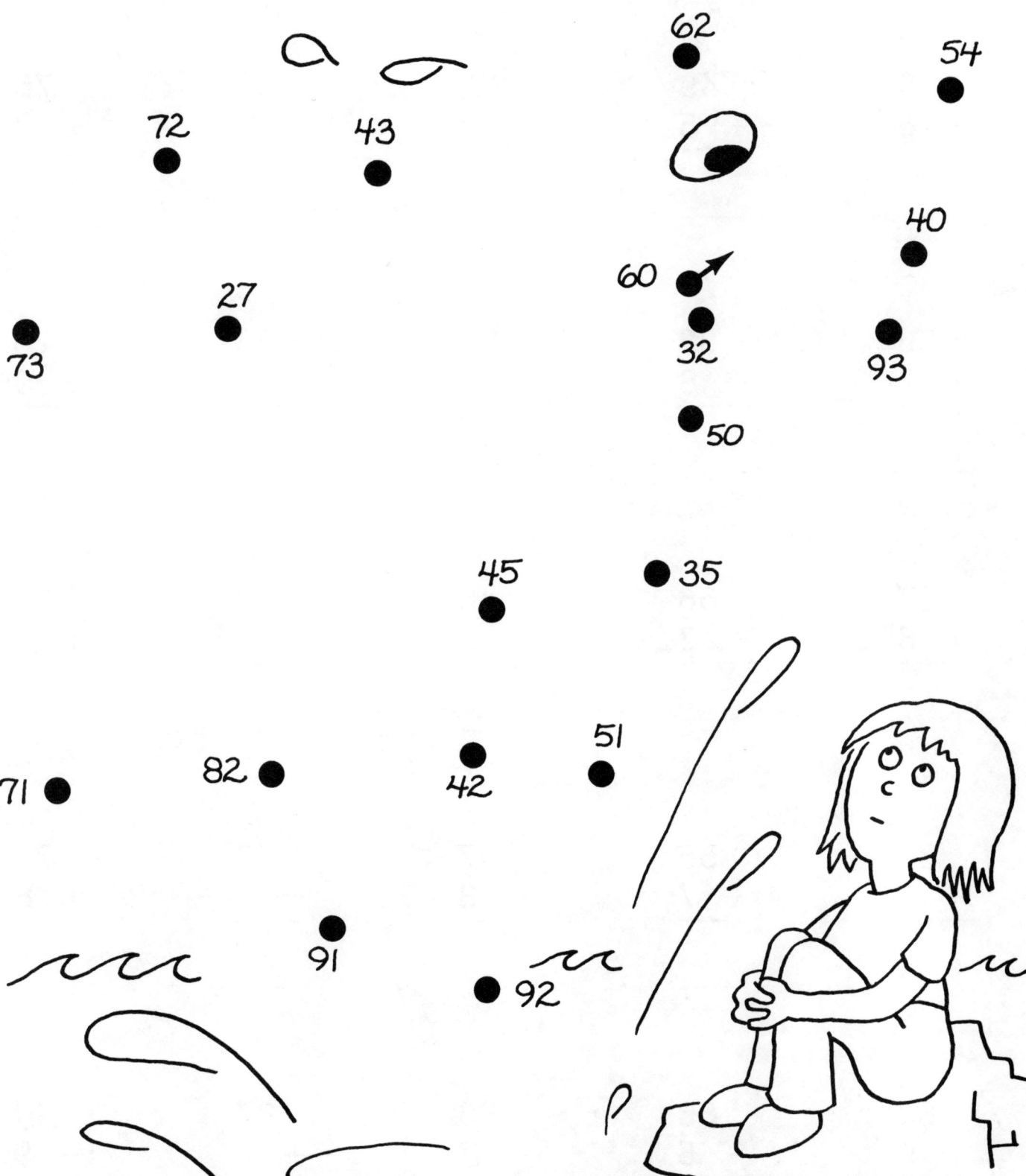

Math-A-Draw Level II

Name _____   Set **24**   Worksheet **A**

Write the correct numeral on each line.

	A	B	C	D	E
1	28 + 6	49 + 5	37 + 7	78 + 4	75 + 9
2	66 + 7	32 + 8	25 + 4	23 + 7	29 + 9
3	27 + 8	56 + 3	46 + 5	68 + 3	43 + 9
4	34 + 8	56 + 7	47 + 8	48 + 1	75 + 8
5	83 + 9	86 + 5	86 + 7	27 + 4	44 + 9

Math-A-Draw Level II

Name _____ Set **24** Worksheet **B**

To find the hidden picture, draw lines from dot to dot. Follow the order of your answers. Start from the dot with the arrow.

Math-A-Draw Level II

Name _____   Set **25** Worksheet **A**

Write the correct numeral on each line.

	A	B	C	D	E
1	68 +15 ____	65 +25 ____	53 +46 ____	39 +49 ____	25 +38 ____
2	44 +36 ____	25 +68 ____	39 +32 ____	19 +67 ____	79 +13 ____
3	45 +28 ____	17 +65 ____	53 +19 ____	38 +53 ____	45 +34 ____
4	47 +23 ____	29 +48 ____	56 +22 ____	57 +19 ____	26 +36 ____

Math-A-Draw Level II

Name _____ Set **25** Worksheet **B**

To find the hidden picture, draw lines from dot to dot. Follow the order of your answers. Start from the dot with the arrow.

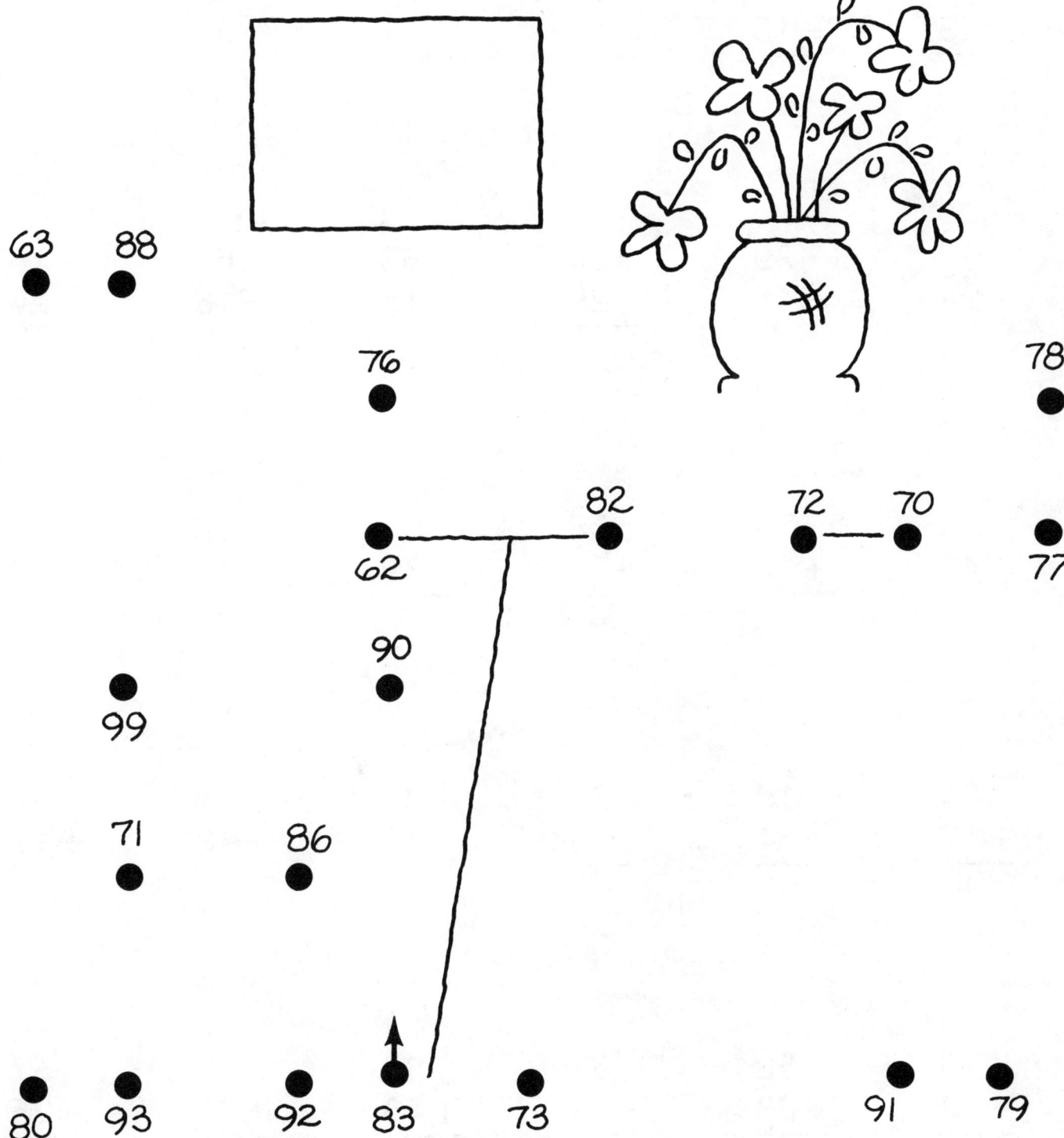

Math-A-Draw Level II

Name _____ Set **26** Worksheet **A**

Write the correct numeral on each line.

	A	B	C	D	E	F
1	29 +23	38 +15	39 +47	79 +17	26 +37	37 +29
2	37 +24	39 +46	59 +29	53 +18	66 +18	13 +26
3	29 +48	78 +16	36 +28	54 +36	28 +48	21 +59
4	64 +17	19 +54	34 +58	32 +59	65 +18	54 +19
5	19 +12	52 +23	67 +26	39 +48	49 +46	57 +25

Math-A-Draw Level II

Name _____ Set **26** Worksheet **B**

To find the hidden picture, draw lines from dot to dot. Follow the order of your answers. Start from the dot with the arrow.

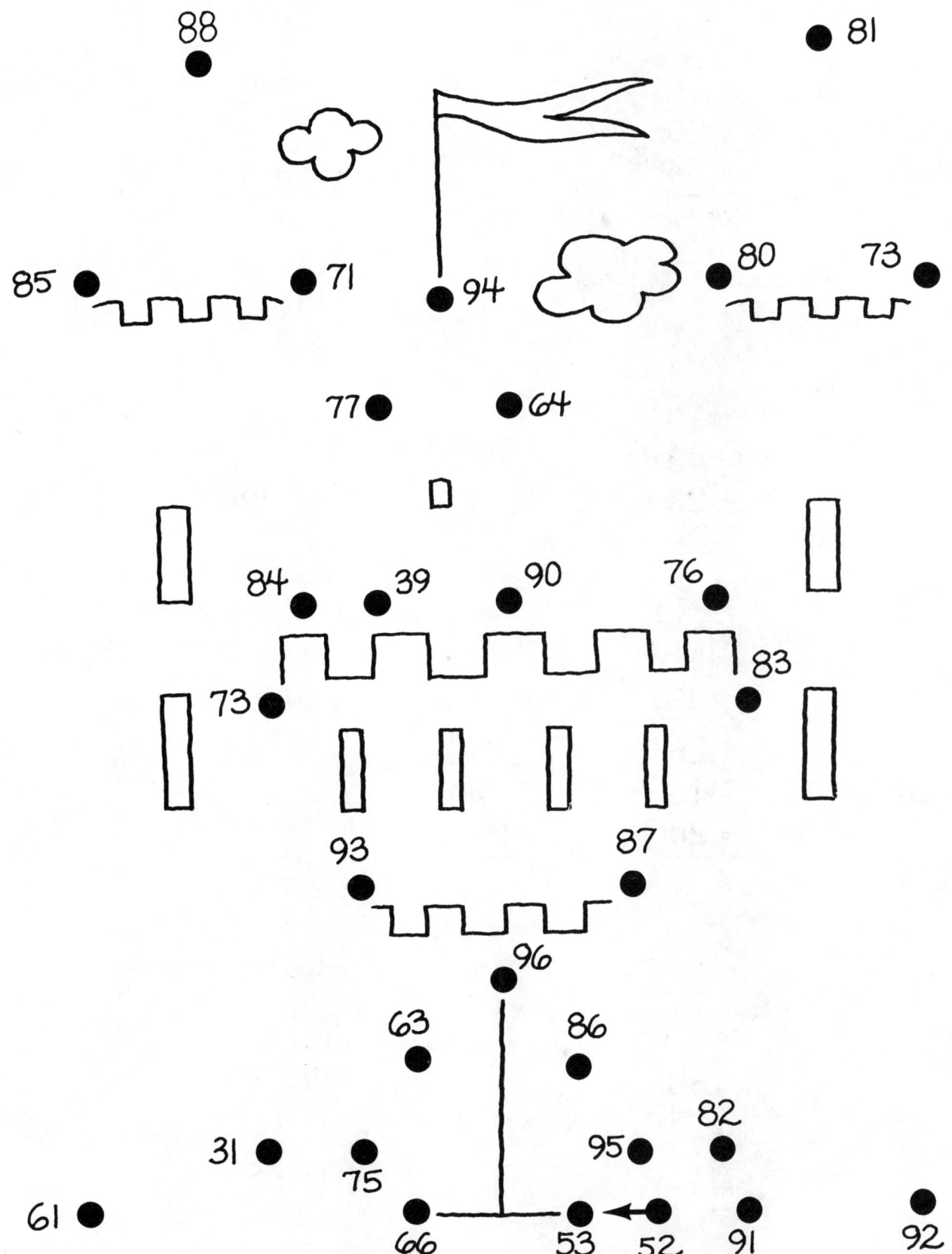

Math-A-Draw Level II

Name _____ Set **27** Worksheet **A**

Write the correct numeral on each line.

	A	B	C	D	E
1	7 27 +35	16 26 +34	15 17 +22	22 4 +59	8 61 +20
2	19 20 +53	9 43 +26	9 40 +12	50 18 +28	24 42 +29
3	10 27 +29	26 13 +24	18 41 + 6	11 7 +37	9 47 +23
4	3 63 +17	68 5 +14	31 6 +47	10 25 +39	30 17 +23

Math-A-Draw Level II

Name _____ Set **27** Worksheet **B**

To find the hidden picture, draw lines from dot to dot. Follow the order of your answers. Start from the dot with the arrow.

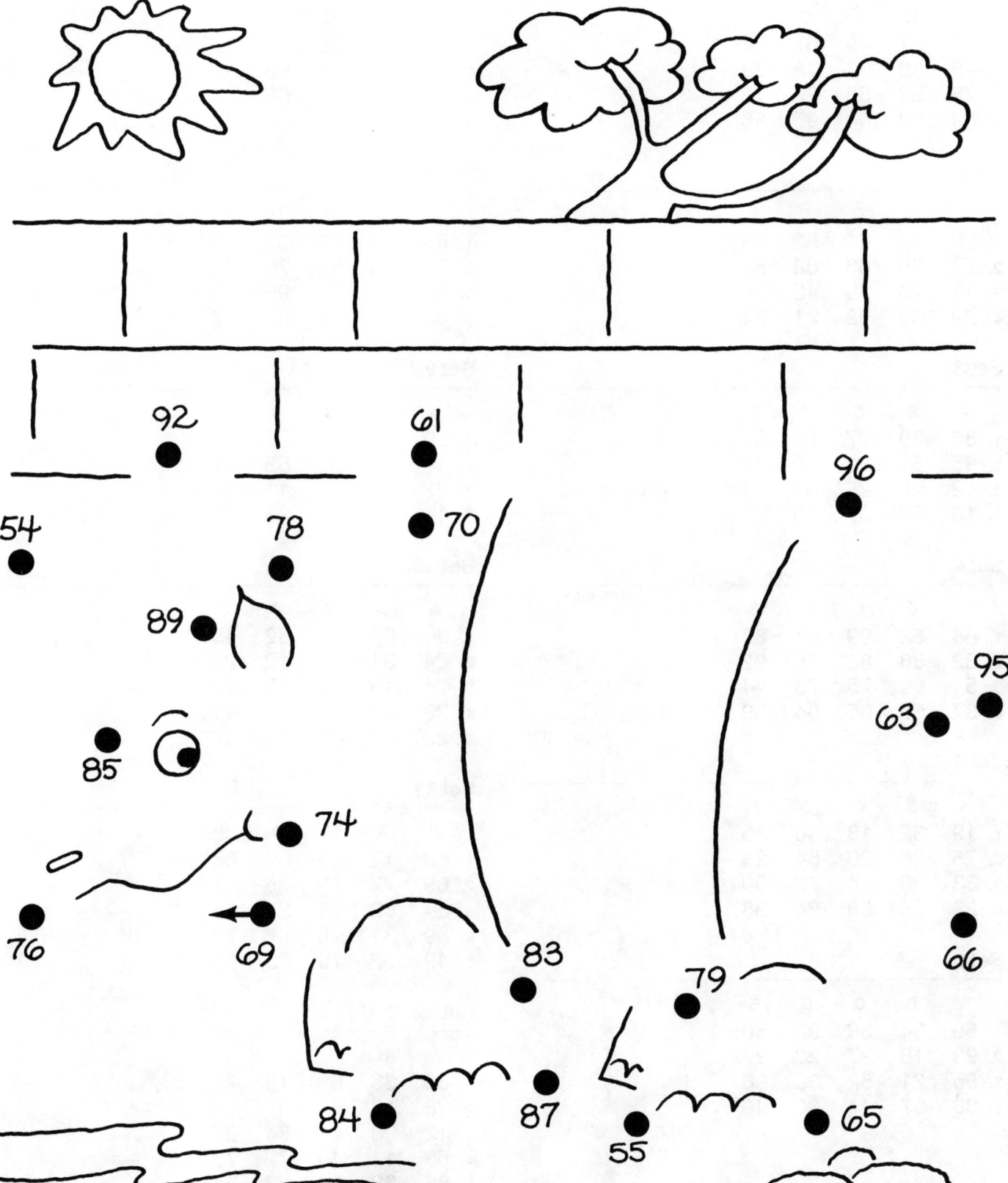

Math-A-Draw Level II

Answer Key

Set 1

	A	B	C	D	E
1.	59	87	49	57	36
2.	48	88	39	19	38
3.	75	26	58	29	78
4.	89	79	44	95	86

Set 2

	A	B	C	D	E
1.	90	60	61	52	53
2.	77	86	63	82	83
3.	41	73	35	40	54
4.	22	32	72	31	81

Set 3

	A	B	C	D	E
1.	86	39	77	94	83
2.	98	31	21	89	78
3.	42	96	25	67	11
4.	19	52	97	85	22

Set 4

	A	B	C	D	E
1.	68	52	99	81	87
2.	82	88	86	65	92
3.	54	89	75	73	44
4.	37	55	95	84	69

Set 5

	A	B	C	D	E
1.	19	32	18	40	16
2.	75	25	20	51	26
3.	33	36	44	17	30
4.	23	28	58	24	38

Set 6

	A	B	C	D	E
1.	56	64	36	92	50
2.	99	18	97	23	27
3.	95	21	62	28	96
4.	33	87	44	85	46

Set 7

	A	B	C	D	E
1.	92	87	73	86	95
2.	84	99	88	93	89
3.	81	65	54	68	83
4.	58	69	96	37	75

Set 8

	A	B	C	D	E
1.	86	98	93	97	75
2.	99	96	58	79	76
3.	89	88	87	95	78
4.	68	69	94	85	77

Set 9

	A	B	C	D	E
1.	20	62	86	55	25
2.	14	32	36	53	41
3.	22	24	13	11	51
4.	16	31	83	23	43

Set 10

	A	B	C	D	E
1.	30	65	61	32	45
2.	24	31	11	12	23
3.	74	13	71	50	15
4.	20	51	80	10	41
5.	22	21	42	17	47

Set 11

	A	B	C	D	E
1.	88	12	99	98	67
2.	69	77	15	36	91
3.	54	62	16	34	57
4.	89	31	79	96	32
5.	49	52	76	85	20

Set 12

	A	B	C	D	E
1.	85	36	89	15	76
2.	78	13	51	97	24
3.	12	26	41	84	27
4.	58	11	46	77	75
5.	86	22	21	87	34

Math-A-Draw Level II

Set 13

	A	B	C	D	E
1.	78	70	51	96	24
2.	22	31	56	69	54
3.	59	45	32	60	68
4.	33	92	99	21	76
5.	43	77	63	89	15

Set 14

	A	B	C	D	E
1.	92	87	73	86	95
2.	84	99	88	93	89
3.	81	65	54	68	83
4.	58	69	96	37	75

Set 15

	A	B	C	D	E
1.	467	489	717	936	584
2.	699	485	388	669	279
3.	908	360	768	419	859
4.	778	865	178	269	579
5.	867	956	299	599	288

Set 16

	A	B	C	D	E
1.	987	949	888	898	978
2.	947	899	377	189	487
3.	926	858	965	847	695
4.	677	975	299	887	489
5.	732	689	796	586	996

Set 17

	A	B	C	D	E
1.	201	112	123	714	477
2.	474	215	142	124	713
3.	948	735	512	383	751
4.	852	645	856	431	242

Set 18

	A	B	C	D	E
1.	20	306	135	123	200
2.	531	134	167	402	340
3.	544	108	35	50	625
4.	29	330	701	114	222

Set 19

	A	B	C	D	E
1.	778	865	956	867	936
2.	279	717	859	649	699
3.	489	579	908	768	584
4.	585	599	467	419	388

Set 20

	A	B	C	D	E
1.	109	59	107	119	108
2.	125	146	98	116	104
3.	157	167	105	122	135
4.	143	127	138	177	168

Set 21

	A	B	C	D	E
1.	103	126	128	108	115
2.	135	114	109	120	146
3.	153	168	177	139	158
4.	143	138	129	165	172

Set 22

	A	B	C	D	E
1.	156	139	125	146	138
2.	149	129	132	167	173
3.	158	164	168	178	126
4.	143	148	177	163	135
5.	145	155	127	168	179

Set 23

	A	B	C	D	E
1.	60	54	62	43	72
2.	73	27	71	64	92
3.	51	91	82	45	42
4.	35	50	93	40	32

Set 24

	A	B	C	D	E
1.	34	54	44	82	84
2.	73	40	29	30	38
3.	35	59	51	71	52
4.	42	63	55	49	83
5.	92	91	93	31	53

Math-A-Draw Level II

Set 25

	A	B	C	D	E
1.	83	90	99	88	63
2.	80	93	71	86	92
3.	73	82	72	91	79
4.	70	77	78	76	62

Set 26

	A	B	C	D	E	F
1.	52	53	86	96	63	66
2.	61	85	88	71	84	39
3.	77	94	64	90	76	80
4.	81	73	92	91	83	73
5.	31	75	93	87	95	82

Set 27

	A	B	C	D	E
1.	69	76	54	85	89
2.	92	78	61	96	95
3.	66	63	65	55	79
4.	83	87	84	74	70

THIS IS

_____

MATH•A•DRAW RECORD.

① ② ③
④ ⑤ ⑥
⑦ ⑧ ⑨
⑩ ⑪ ⑫
⑬ ⑭ ⑮
⑯ ⑰ ⑱
⑲ ⑳ ㉑
㉒ ㉓ ㉔
㉕ ㉖ ㉗

Congratulations

_____

**for excellence in
MATH•A•DRAW**

_____
TEACHER

_____
DATE

Math-A-Draw Level II

Math·A·Draw

Level III · Subtraction for Grades 2–4

27 dot-to-dot math learning games
sequenced according to level of difficulty

Contents

Subtraction from 10 with checking. Regrouping in one's place.   Sets **1** and **2**

Subtraction from 10 with checking. Regrouping in one's and ten's places.   Set **3**

Subtraction from 11 with checking. Regrouping in one's place.   Sets **4** and **5**

Subtraction from 11 with checking. Regrouping in one's and ten's places.   Set **6**

Review of subtraction from 10 and 11 with checking. Regrouping in one's and ten's places.   Set **7**

Subtraction from 12 with checking. Mixed regrouping.   Sets **8–10**

Review of subtraction from 10, 11, and 12 with checking. Mixed regrouping.   Set **11**

Subtraction from 13 with checking. Mixed regrouping.   Sets **12–14**

Review of subtraction from 10, 11, 12, and 13 with checking. Mixed regrouping.   Sets **15** and **16**

Subtraction from 14 with checking. Mixed regrouping.   Sets **17–19**

Review of subtraction from 10, 11, 12, 13, and 14 with checking. Mixed regrouping.   Set **20**

Subtraction from 15, 16, 17, and 18. Mixed regrouping.   Sets **21** and **22**

Subtraction from zero with checking. Zero in ten's place.   Set **23**

Math-A-Draw Level III

Subtraction from zero with checking. Zero in one's and ten's places.   Sets **24** and **25**

Subtraction from zero with checking. Zero in one's, ten's, and hundred's places.   Sets **26** and **27**

Answer Key

Record Card and Certificate

Name _____ Set **1** Worksheet **A**

**Answer each subtraction problem.
Then, check it by addition.**

	A	B	C	D	E	F
1	70 − 4 = 66	66 + 4 = 70	20 − 12 =	+ 12 = 20	40 − 29 =	+ 29 = 40
2	60 − 39 =	+ 39 =	30 − 18 =	+ 18 =	80 − 43 =	+ 43 =
3	50 − 33 =	+ 33 =	90 − 89 =	+ 89 =	10 − 7 =	+ 7 =
4	350 − 35 =	+ 35 =	270 − 62 =	+ 62 =	190 − 87 =	+ 87 =
5	250 − 9 =	+ 9 =	380 − 58 =	+ 58 =	260 − 43 =	+ 43 =
6	150 − 40 =	+ 40 =	450 − 204 =	+ 204 =	390 − 127 =	+ 127 =

Math-A-Draw Level III

Name _____ Set **1** Worksheet **B**

To find the hidden picture, draw lines from dot to dot. Follow the order of your answers. Start from the dot with the arrow.

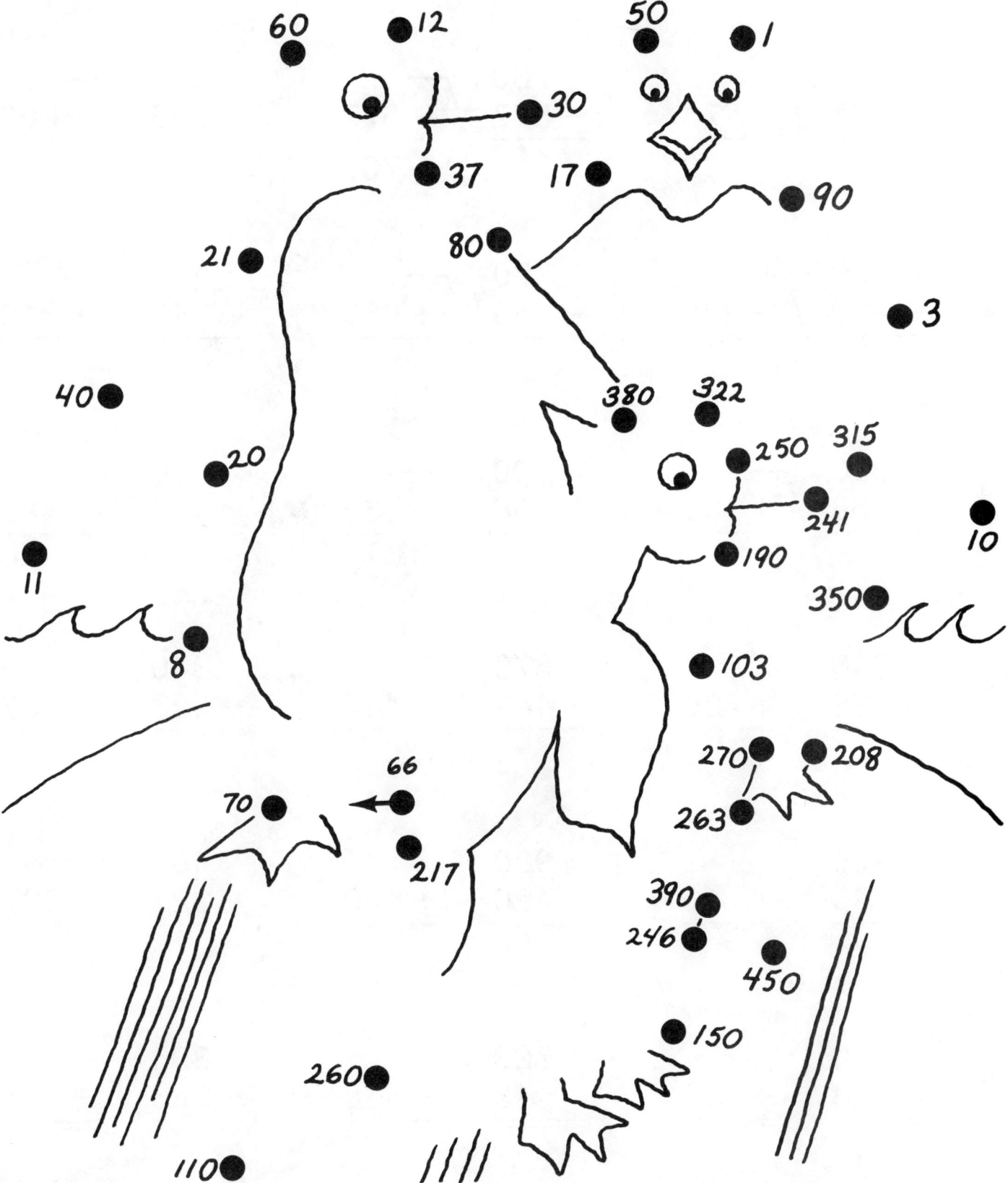

Math-A-Draw Level III

Name _____   Set **2** Worksheet **A**

**Answer each subtraction problem.
Then, check it by addition.**

	A	B	C	D	E	F
1	180 − 73	+ 73 → 180	780 − 577	+ 577 → 780	580 − 268	+ 268
2	450 − 230	+ 230	770 − 658	+ 658	320 − 13	+ 13
3	690 − 68	+ 68	990 − 36	+ 36	840 − 420	+ 420
4	640 − 339	+ 339	670 − 447	+ 447	340 − 23	+ 23
5	160 − 45	+ 45	930 − 420	+ 420	480 − 327	+ 327
6	350 − 223	+ 223	720 − 18	+ 18	390 − 266	+

Math-A-Draw Level III

Name _____ Set **2** Worksheet **B**

To find the hidden picture, draw lines from dot to dot. Follow the order of your answers. Start from the dot with the arrow.

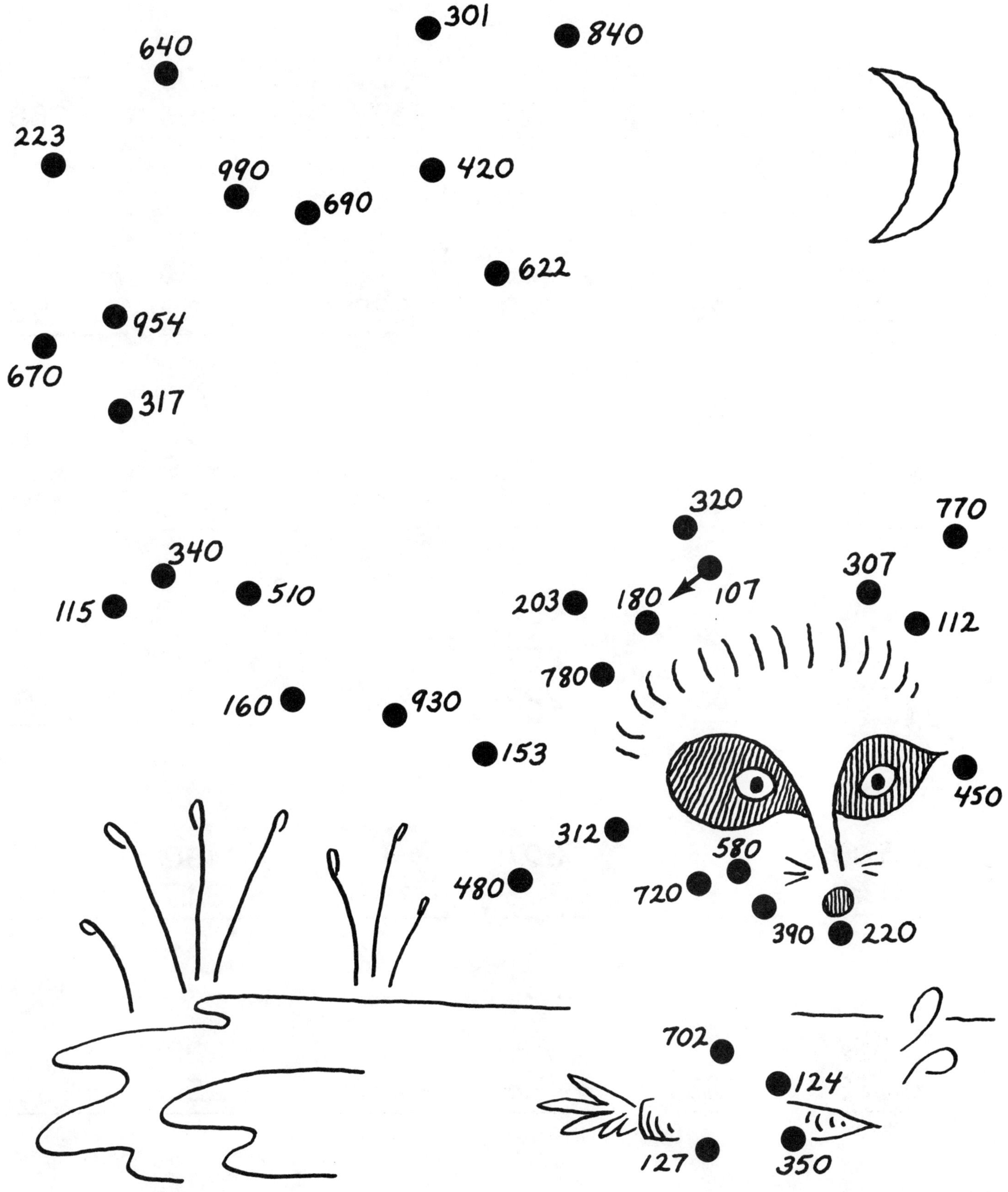

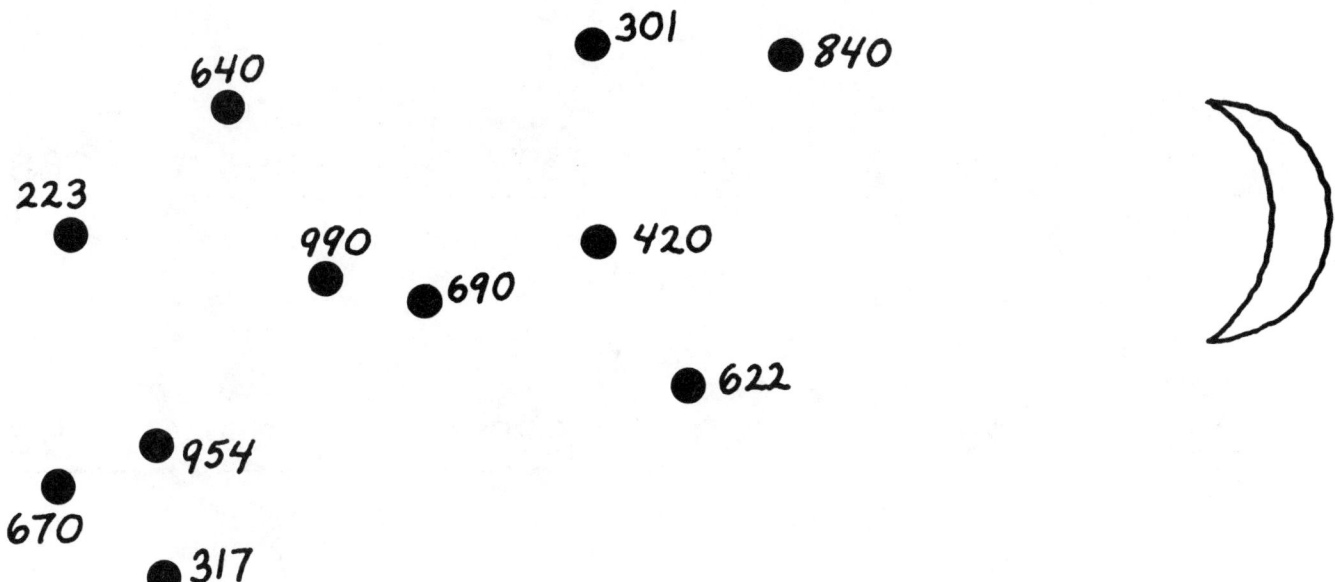

Math-A-Draw Level III

Name _____ Set 3   Worksheet A

**Answer each subtraction problem.
Then, check it by addition.**

	A	B	C	D	E	F

1.   300   + 80   800   +   806   + 365
   − 80   − 790   − 365

2.   920   + 815   720   + 520   660   + 59
   − 815   − 520   − 59

3.   808   + 755   640   + 27   509   + 378
   − 755   − 27   − 378

4.   707   + 463   807   + 222   409   + 76
   − 463   − 222   − 76

5.   530   + 324   307   + 193   490   + 349
   − 324   − 193   − 349

6.   709   + 93   540   +   990   + 250
   − 93   − 26   − 250

Math-A-Draw Level III

Name _____ Set **3** Worksheet **B**

To find the hidden picture, draw lines from dot to dot. Follow the order of your answers. Start from the dot with the arrow.

Math-A-Draw Level III

Name _____   Set 4   Worksheet **A**

**Answer each subtraction problem.
Then, check it by addition.**

	A	B	C	D	E	F
1	51 − 3	+ 3	81 − 6	+ 6	61 − 60	+ 60
2	71 − 66	+ 66	91 − 56	+ 56	31 − 21	+ 21
3	41 − 16	+ 16	221 − 15	+ 15	181 − 30	+ 30
4	691 − 65	+ 65	391 − 8	+ 8	571 − 24	+ 24
5	341 − 25	+ 25	321 − 15	+ 15	191 − 85	+ 85
6	681 − 4	+ 4	351 − 40	+ 40	781 − 36	+ 36

Math-A-Draw Level III

Name _____   Set **4** Worksheet **B**

To find the hidden picture, draw lines from dot to dot. Follow the order of your answers. Start from the dot with the arrow.

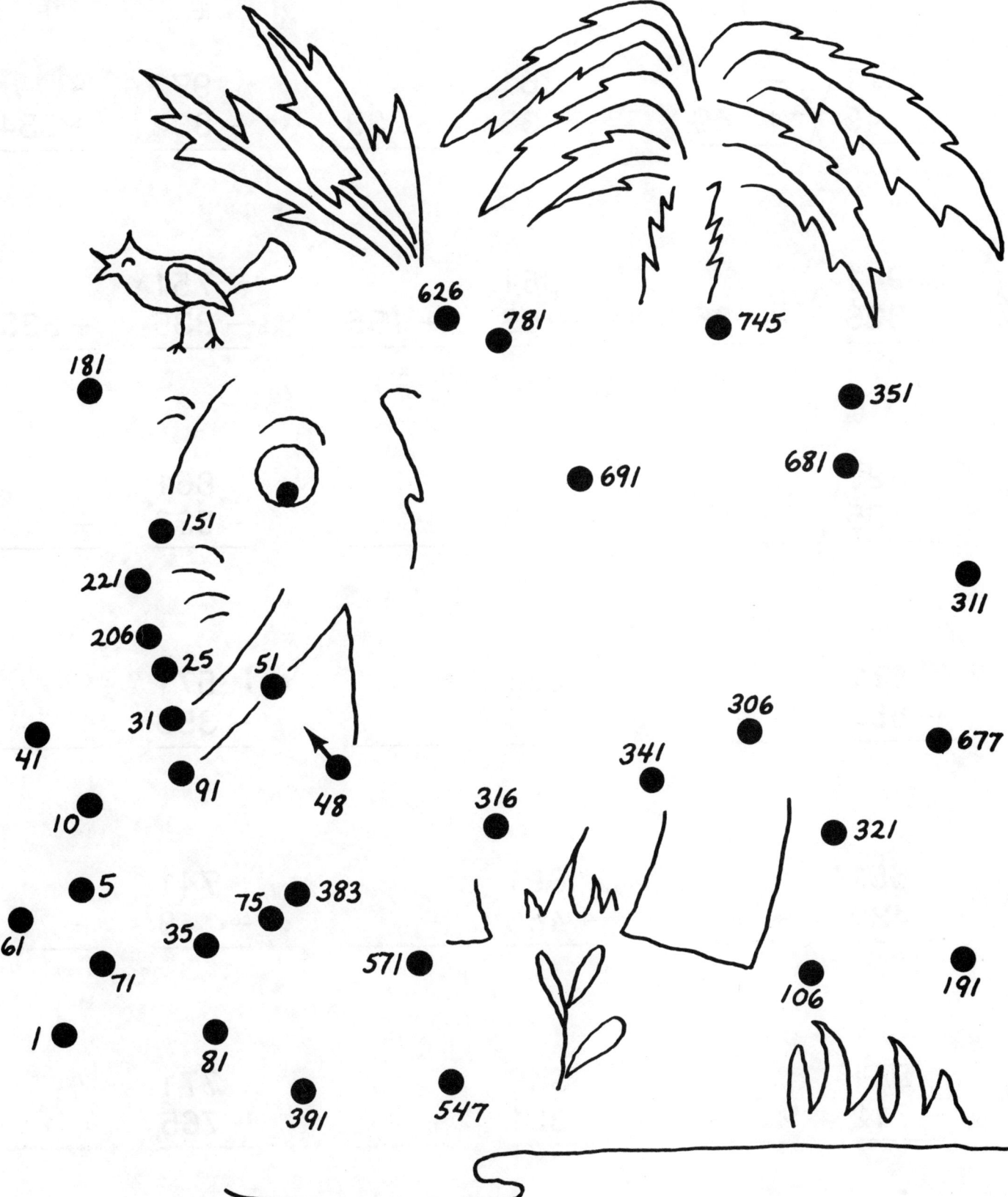

Math-A-Draw Level III

Name _____   Set 5   Worksheet **A**

**Answer each subtraction problem.
Then, check it by addition.**

	A	B	C	D	E	F
1	991 − 49	+ 49	761 − 33	+ 33	971 − 834	+ 834
2	941 − 326	+ 326	361 − 155	+ 155	751 − 335	+ 335
3	821 − 805	+	961 − 53	+	861 − 532	+
4	871 − 555	+	851 − 4	+	571 − 356	+
5	651 − 430	+	891 − 465	+	741 − 8	+
6	841 − 712	+	946 − 321	+	771 − 765	+

Math-A-Draw Level III

Name _____ Set **5** Worksheet **B**

To find the hidden picture, draw lines from dot to dot. Follow the order of your answers. Start from the dot with the arrow.

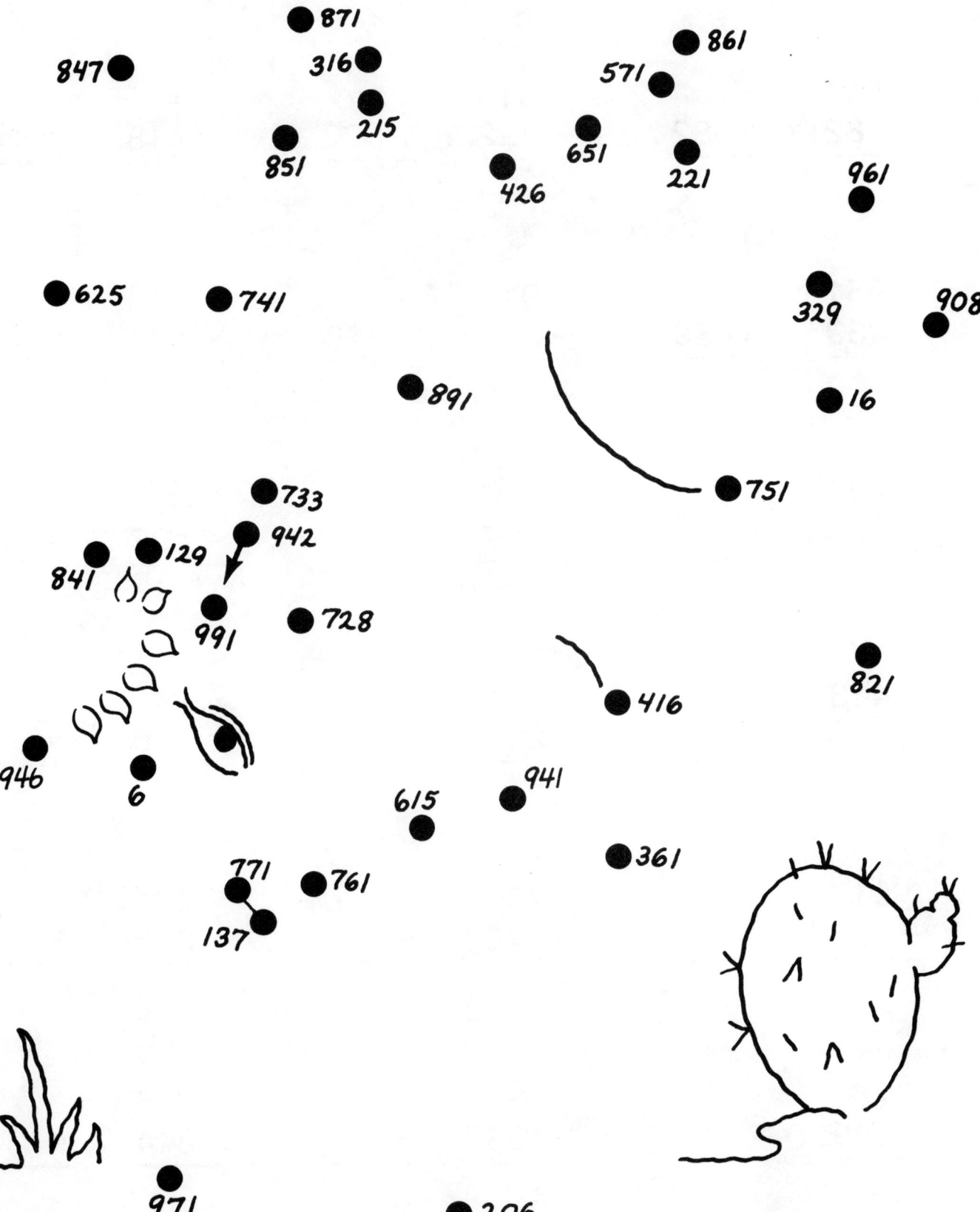

Math-A-Draw Level III

Name _____ Set 6 Worksheet **A**

**Answer each subtraction problem.
Then, check it by addition.**

	A	B	C	D	E	F
1	814 − 82	+ 82	915 − 322	+ 322	121 − 18	+ 18
2	951 − 439	+ 439	919 − 368	+ 368	816 − 423	+ 423
3	881 − 28	+	918 − 97	+	431 − 407	+
4	413 − 333	+	841 − 227	+	941 − 538	+
5	917 − 57	+	791 − 76	+	491 − 255	+
6	751 − 329	+	831 − 408	+	615 − 244	+

Math-A-Draw Level III

Name _____   Set **6** Worksheet **B**

To find the hidden picture, draw lines from dot to dot. Follow the order of your answers. Start from the dot with the arrow.

Math-A-Draw Level III

Name _____

Set **7**   Worksheet **A**
Review: Subtraction from 10 and 11.

Answer each subtraction problem.
Then, check it by addition.

	A	B	C	D	E	F
1	813 − 263	+ 263	410 − 106	+ 106	819 − 493	+ 493
2	708 − 444	+ 444	690 − 587	+ 587	408 − 36	+ 36
3	911 − 602	+	806 − 533	+	891 − 780	+
4	905 − 71	+	580 − 324	+	913 − 803	+
5	341 − 227	+	431 − 17	+	816 − 95	+
6	709 − 86	+	999 − 645	+	718 − 96	+

Math-A-Draw Level III

Name _____   Set **7** Worksheet **B**

To find the hidden picture, draw lines from dot to dot. Follow the order of your answers. Start from the dot with the arrow.

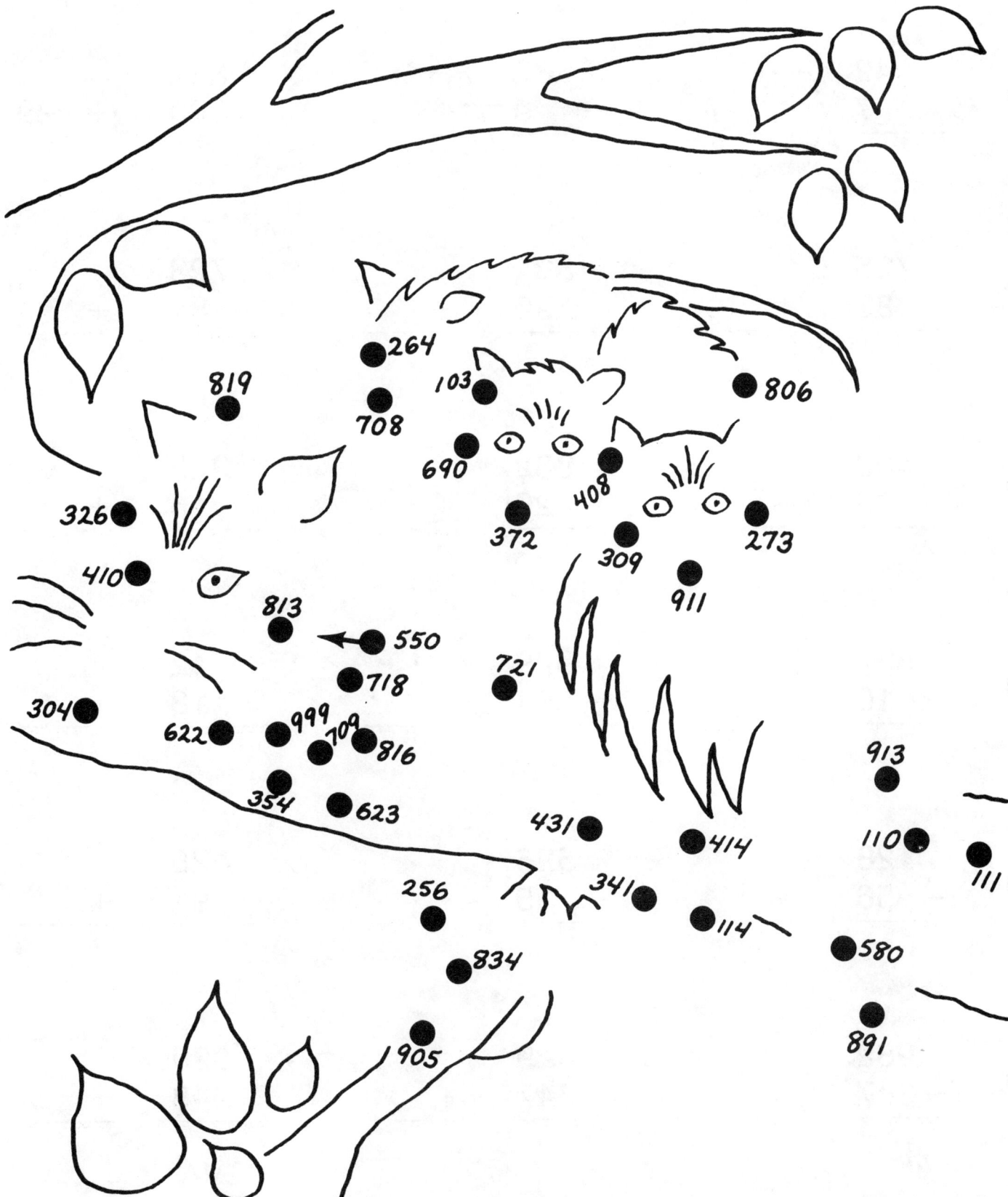

Math-A-Draw Level III

Name _____ Set **8** Worksheet **A**

**Answer each subtraction problem.
Then, check it by addition.**

	A	B	C	D	E	F
1	42 − 7	+ 7	32 − 9	+ 9	342 − 29	+ 29
2	725 − 82	+	821 − 90	+	723 − 81	+
3	462 − 29	+	832 − 29	+	322 − 15	+
4	522 − 10	+	629 − 94	+	742 − 18	+
5	128 − 56	+	526 − 35	+	425 − 91	+
6	982 − 347	+	529 − 347	+	329 − 248	+

Math-A-Draw Level III

Name _____ Set **8** Worksheet **B**

To find the hidden picture, draw lines from dot to dot. Follow the order of your answers. Start from the dot with the arrow.

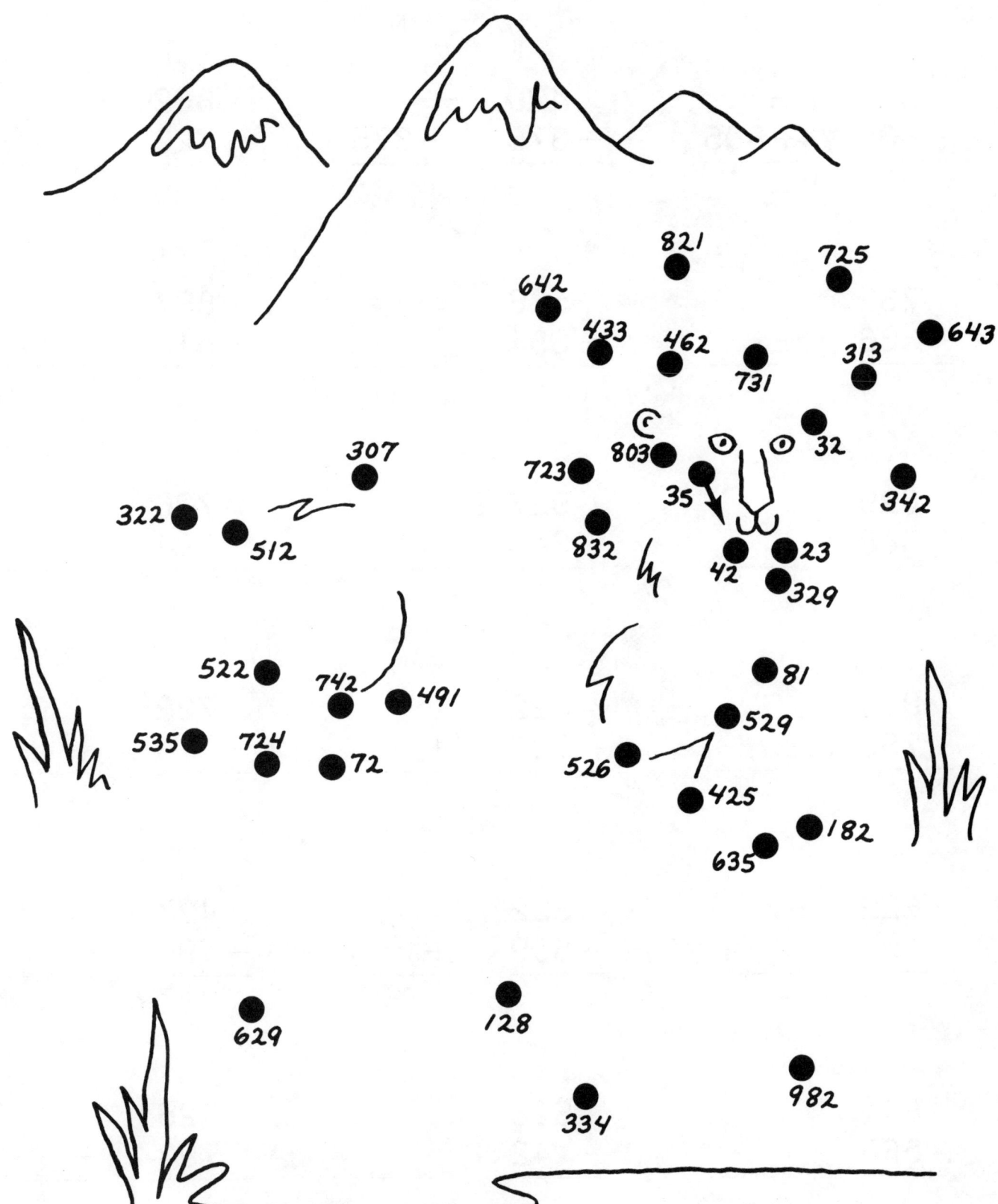

Math-A-Draw Level III

Name _____   Set **9** Worksheet **A**

**Answer each subtraction problem.
Then, check it by addition.**

	A	B	C	D	E	F
1	922 − 805	+ 805	429 − 375	+ 375	852 − 729	+ 729
2	782 − 566	+	526 − 384	+	827 − 516	+
3	629 − 568	+	927 − 645	+	726 − 594	+
4	829 − 758	+	322 − 206	+	722 − 10	+
5	622 − 91	+	822 − 509	+	427 − 95	+
6	821 − 560	+	326 − 42	+	825 − 793	+

Math-A-Draw Level III

Name _____ Set **9** Worksheet **B**

To find the hidden picture, draw lines from dot to dot. Follow the order of your answers. Start from the dot with the arrow.

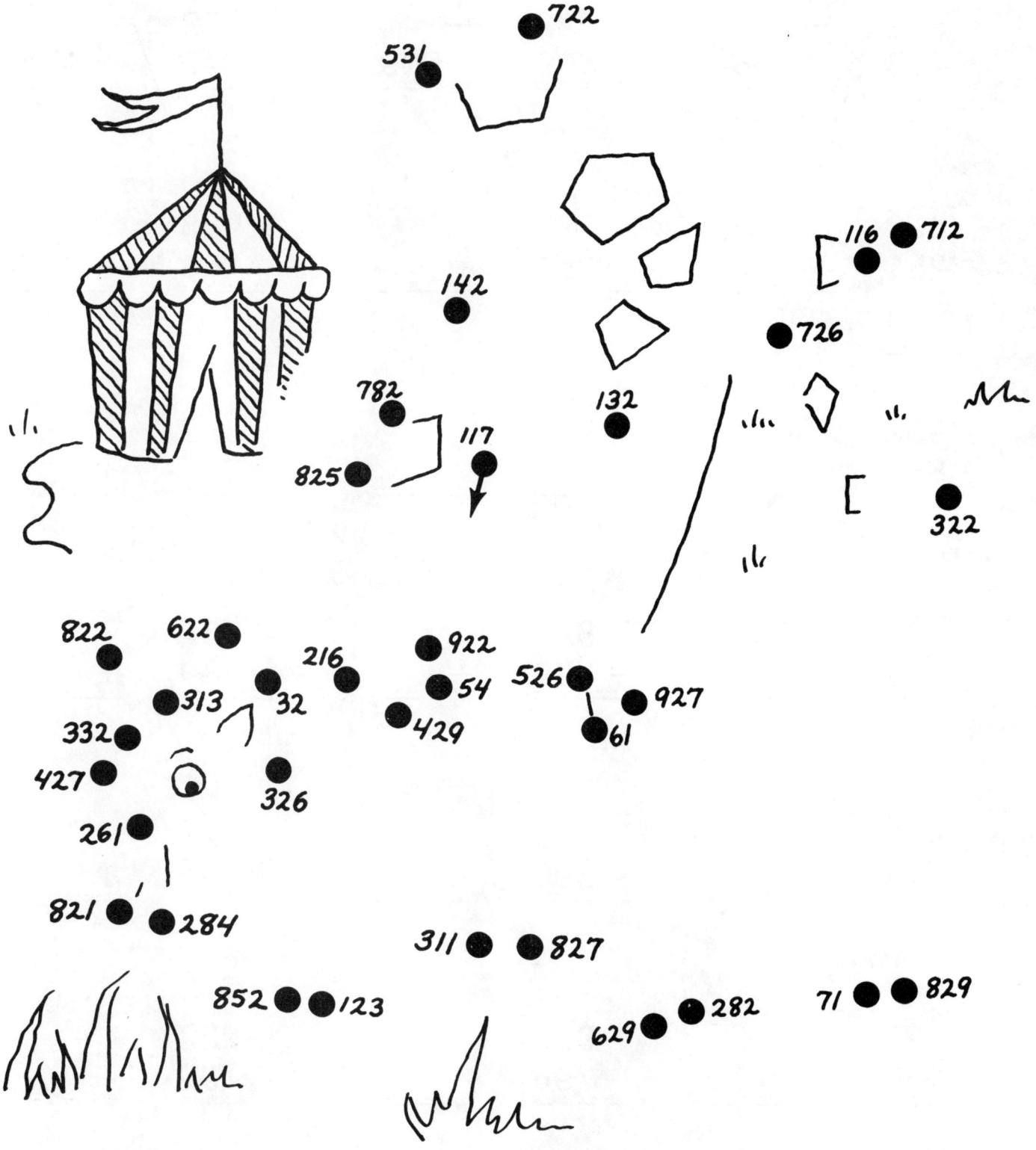

Math-A-Draw Level III

Name _____ Set **10** Worksheet **A**

**Answer each subtraction problem.
Then, check it by addition.**

	A	B	C	D	E	F
1	832 − 486	+ 486	722 − 509	+ 509	752 − 647	+ 647
2	422 − 281	+	727 − 354	+	928 − 465	+
3	932 − 869	+	432 − 267	+	982 − 345	+
4	972 − 765	+	822 − 590	+	332 − 289	+
5	829 − 59	+	622 − 399	+	522 − 496	+
6	322 − 169	+	922 − 796	+	222 − 95	+

Math-A-Draw Level III

Name _____ Set **10** Worksheet **B**

To find the hidden picture, draw lines from dot to dot. Follow the order of your answers. Start from the dot with the arrow.

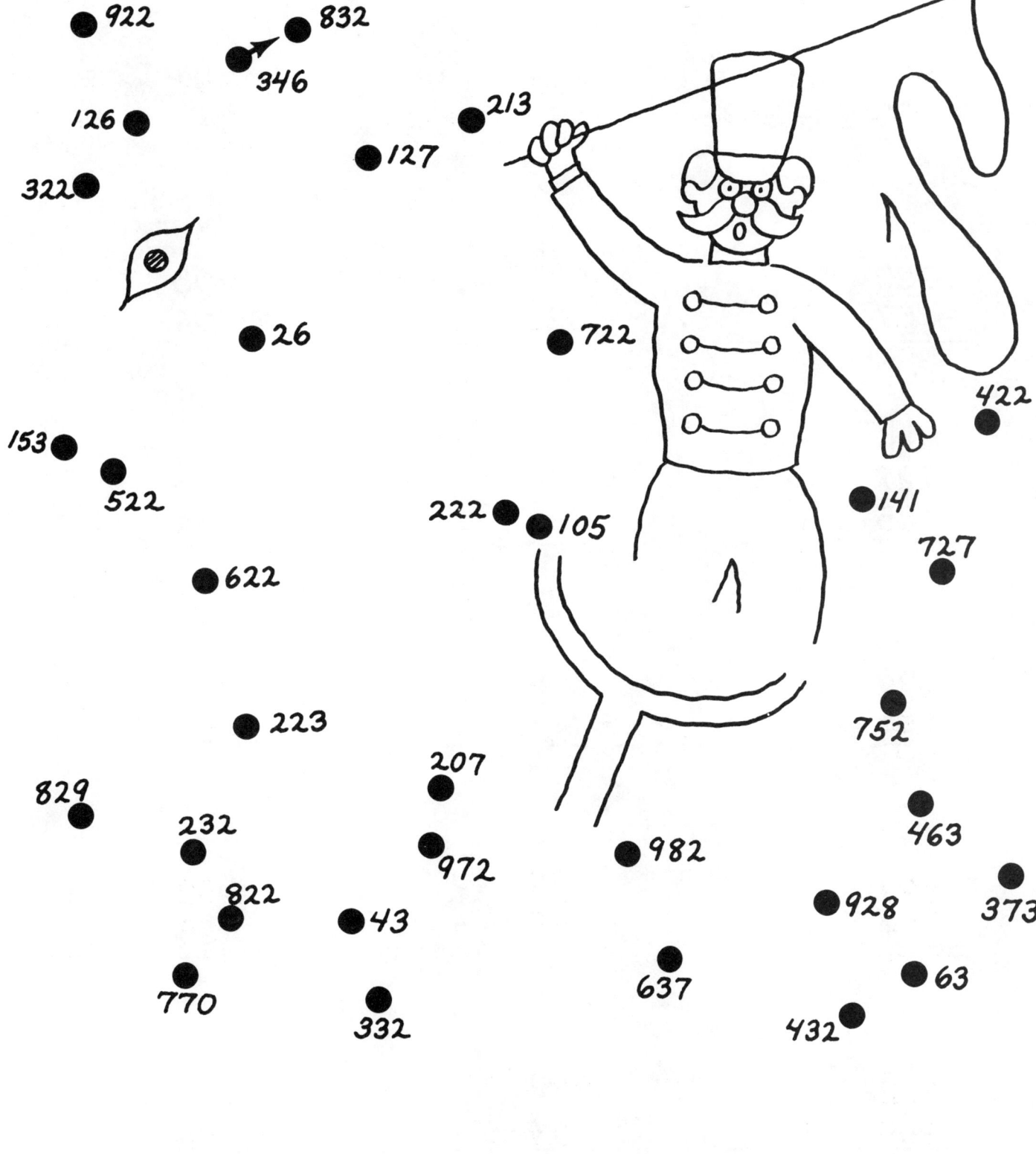

Math-A-Draw Level III

Name _____

Set **11** Worksheet **A**
Review: Subtraction from 10, 11, and 12.

Answer each subtraction problem.
Then, check it by addition.

	A	B	C	D	E	F
1	509 − 398	+ 398	927 − 45	+	491 − 173	+
2	790 − 67	+	832 − 524	+	605 − 94	+
3	727 − 485	+	829 − 492	+	914 − 884	+
4	690 − 285	+	808 − 308	+	426 − 134	+
5	481 − 277	+	709 − 635	+	982 − 463	+
6	437 − 325	+	992 − 47	+	729 − 65	+

Math-A-Draw Level III

Name _____ Set **11** Worksheet **B**

To find the hidden picture, draw lines from dot to dot. Follow the order of your answers. Start from the dot with the arrow.

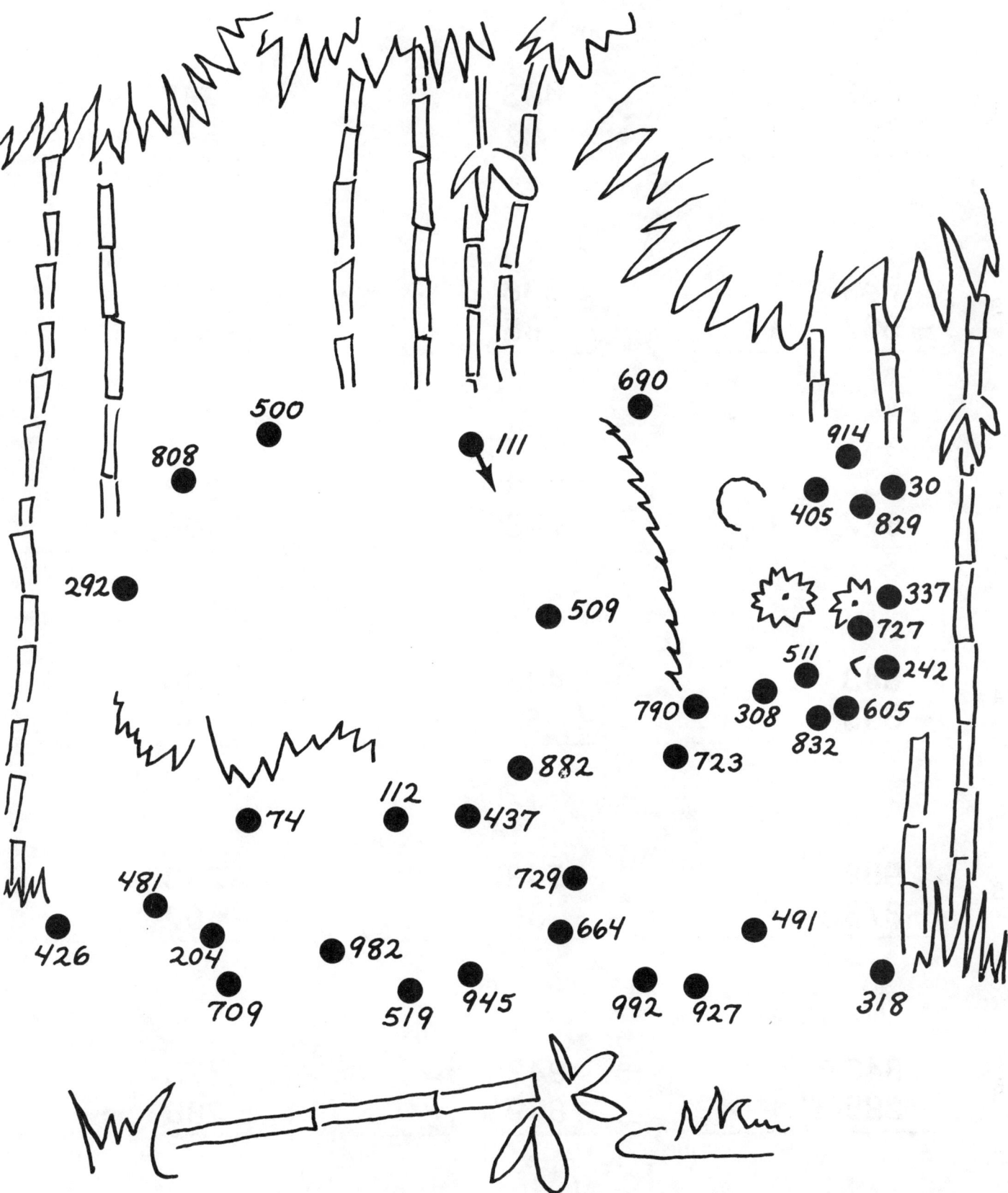

Math-A-Draw Level III

Name _____ Set **12** Worksheet **A**

**Answer each subtraction problem.
Then, check it by addition.**

	A	B	C	D	E	F
1	763 − 559	+	493 − 87	+	743 − 695	+
2	749 − 537	+	536 − 85	+	643 − 429	+
3	933 − 877	+	893 − 786	+	863 − 156	+
4	843 − 695	+	443 − 55	+	939 − 86	+
5	938 − 878	+	543 − 89	+	243 − 67	+
6	343 − 285	+	943 − 879	+	473 − 236	+

Math-A-Draw Level III

Name _____   Set **12** Worksheet **B**

To find the hidden picture, draw lines from dot to dot. Follow the order of your answers. Start from the dot with the arrow.

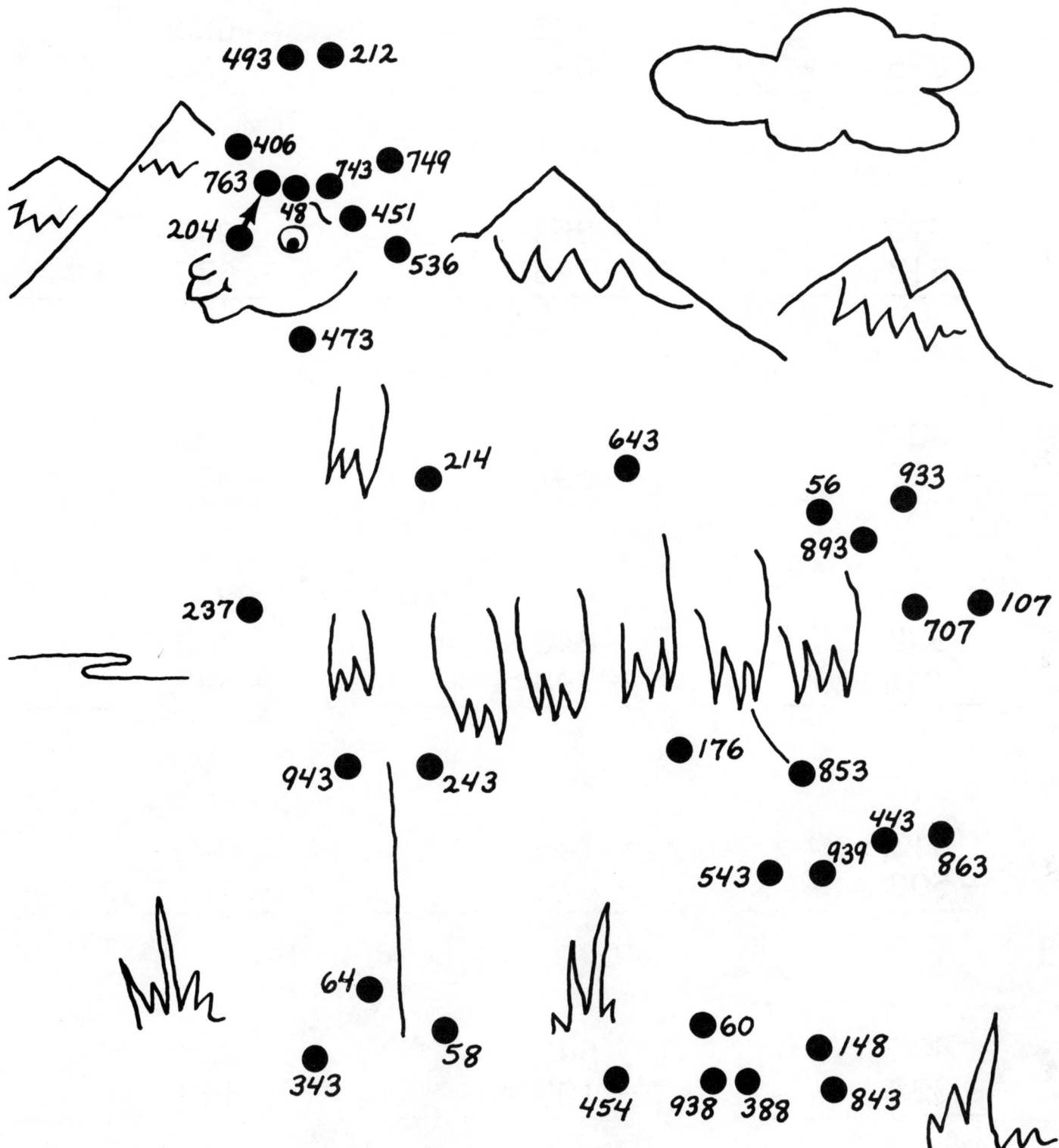

Math-A-Draw Level III

Name _____ Set **13** Worksheet **A**

**Answer each subtraction problem.
Then, check it by addition.**

	A	B	C	D	E	F
1	883 − 255	+ ___	833 − 691	+ ___	633 − 334	+ ___
2	723 − 617	+ ___	863 − 745	+ ___	943 − 576	+ ___
3	634 − 522	+ ___	733 − 597	+ ___	623 − 465	+ ___
4	532 − 461	+ ___	843 − 798	+ ___	739 − 695	+ ___
5	613 − 506	+ ___	743 − 676	+ ___	643 − 468	+ ___
6	435 − 392	+ ___	543 − 196	+ ___	233 − 197	+ ___

Math-A-Draw Level III

Name _____ Set **13** Worksheet **B**

To find the hidden picture, draw lines from dot to dot. Follow the order of your answers. Start from the dot with the arrow.

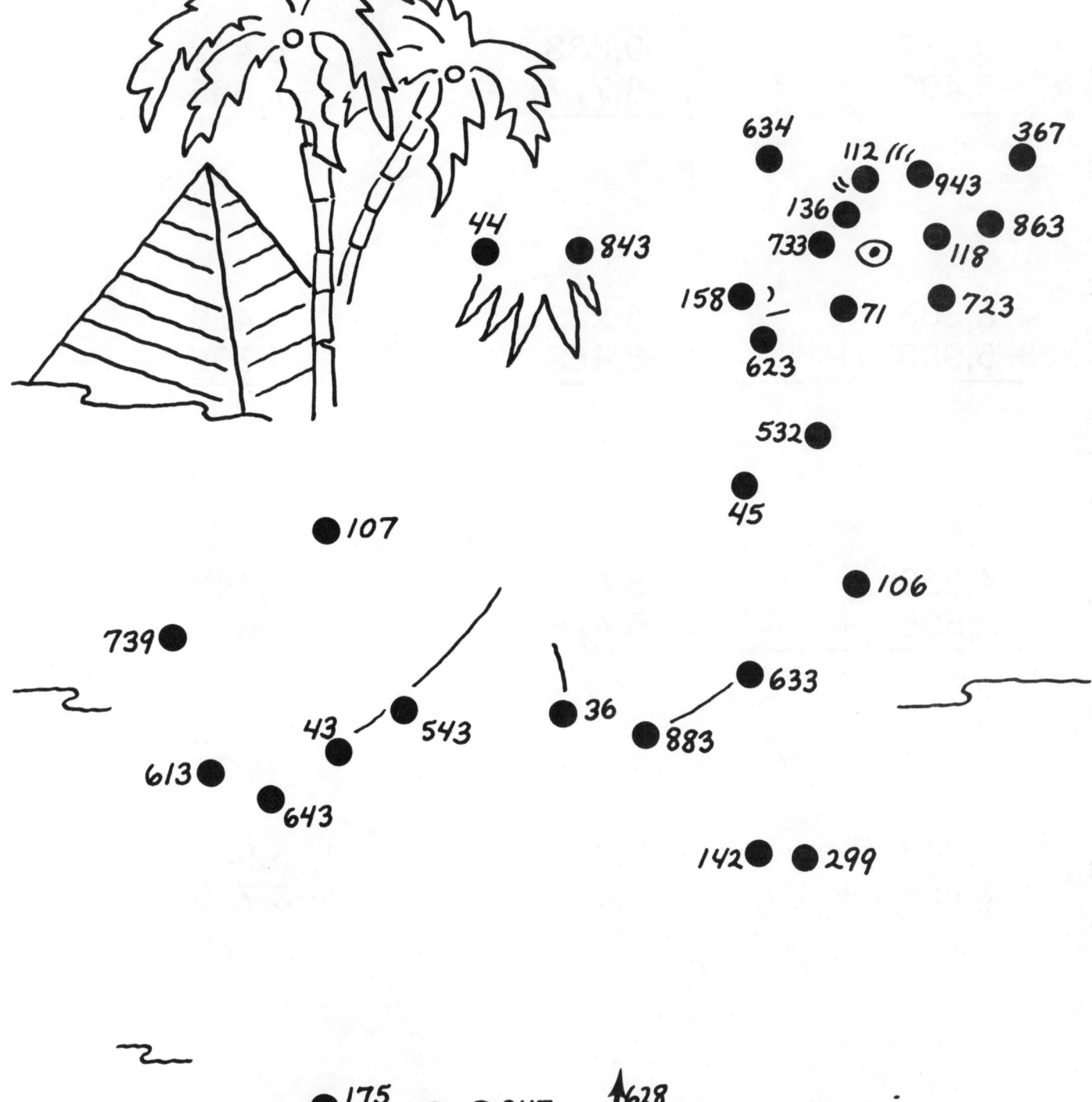

Math-A-Draw Level III

Name _____   Set **14** Worksheet **A**

Answer each subtraction problem.
Then, check it by addition.

	A	B	C	D	E	F
1	9,337 −6,486	+	9,333 −8,777	+	8,432 −7,695	+
2	8,338 −5,986	+	5,233 −3,459	+	9,438 −6,595	+
3	4,339 −2,895	+	8,633 −5,478	+	6,443 −5,699	+
4	4,343 −3,928	+	3,437 −2,985	+	5,832 −3,729	+
5	6,389 −5,965	+	5,329 −4,698	+	3,443 −1,686	+

Math-A-Draw Level III

Name _____ Set **14** Worksheet **B**

To find the hidden picture, draw lines from dot to dot. Follow the order of your answers. Start from the dot with the arrow.

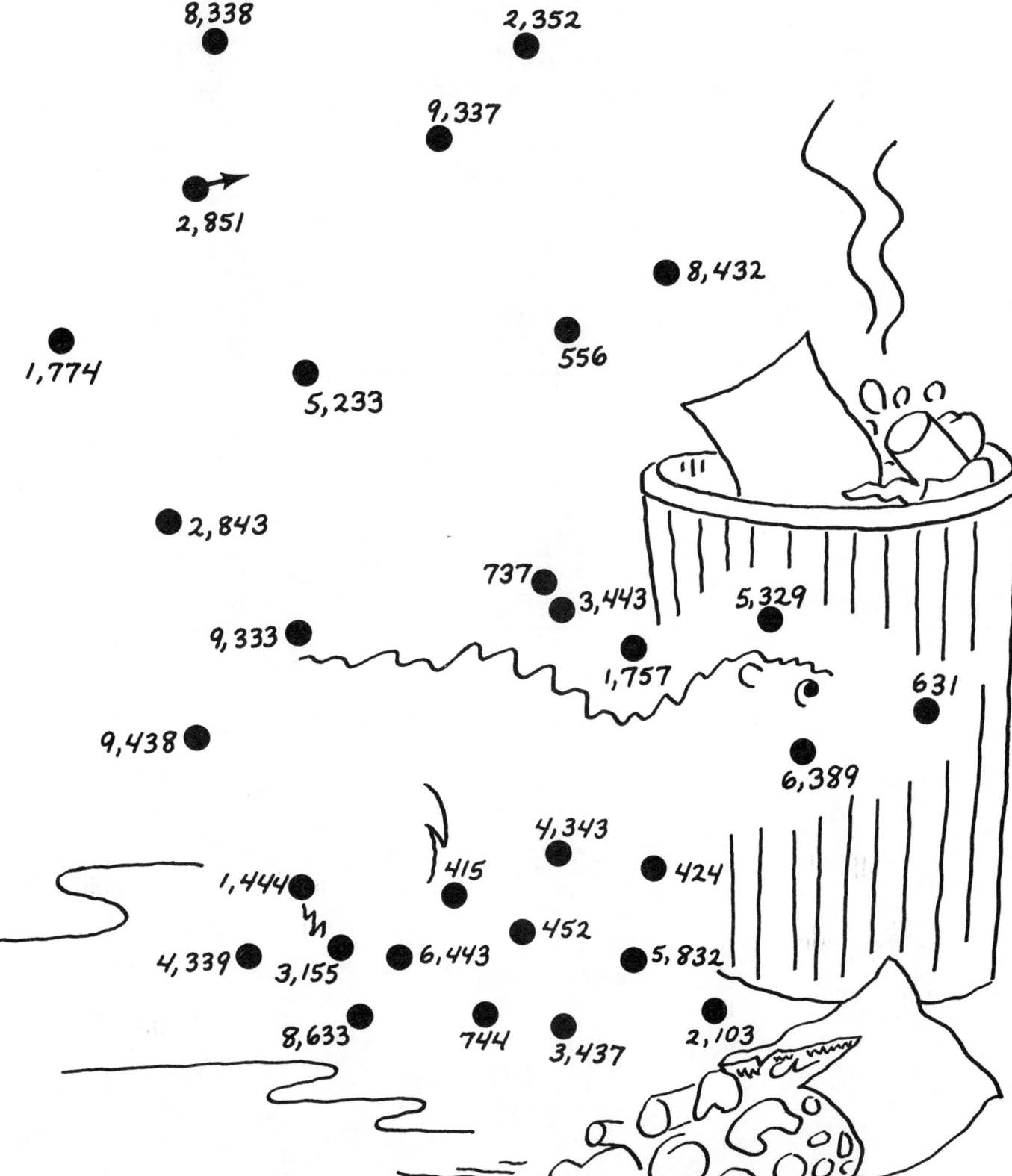

Math-A-Draw Level III

Name _____

Set **15** Worksheet **A**
Review: Subtraction from 10, 11, 12, and 13.

Answer each subtraction problem.
Then, check it by addition.

	A	B	C	D	E	F
1	4,093 −2,874	+	9,233 −5,678	+	8,231 −　597	+
2	8,047 −5,843	+	6,310 −5,497	+	3,143 −2,958	+
3	4,038 −3,456	+	7,893 −7,682	+	8,137 −6,596	+
4	5,393 −　428	+	9,832 −9,076	+	7,940 −5,878	+
5	8,295 −4,952	+	4,309 −2,893	+	6,429 −　752	+

Math-A-Draw Level III

Name _____ Set **15** Worksheet **B**

To find the hidden picture, draw lines from dot to dot. Follow the order of your answers. Start from the dot with the arrow.

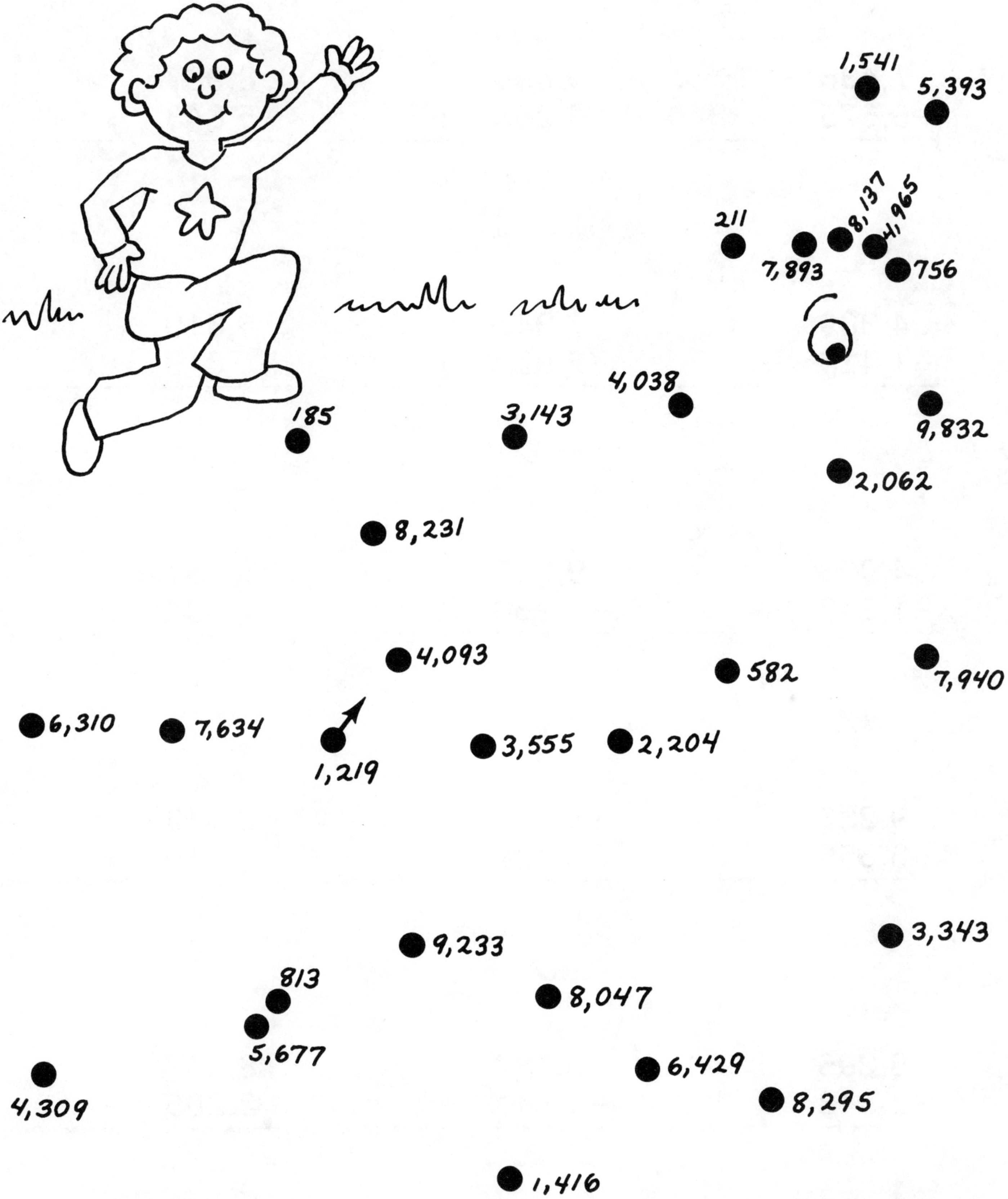

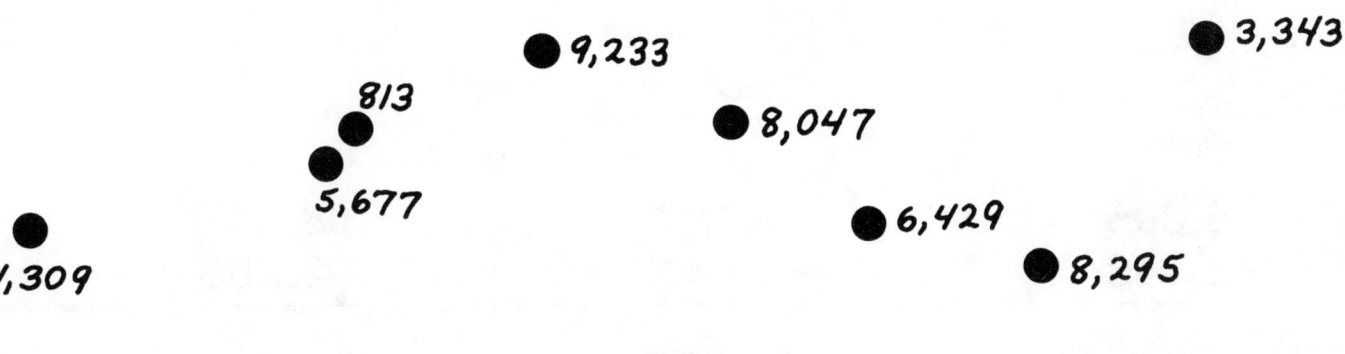

Math-A-Draw Level III

Name _____

Set 16   Worksheet A
Review: Subtraction from 10, 11, 12, and 13.

**Answer each subtraction problem.
Then, check it by addition.**

	A	B	C	D	E	F
1	7,436 −5,675	+	9,695 −6,263	+	8,937 −5,843	+
2	4,309 −1,416	+	7,940 −2,062	+	6,310 − 813	+
3	4,093 −1,219	+	9,389 −7,256	+	8,231 −7,634	+
4	9,233 −3,555	+	5,393 − 428	+	3,143 − 175	+
5	8,295 −3,343	+	8,137 −1,541	+	8,047 −2,205	+

Math-A-Draw Level III

Name _____ Set **16** Worksheet **B**

To find the hidden picture, draw lines from dot to dot. Follow the order of your answers. Start from the dot with the arrow.

Math-A-Draw Level III

Name _____   Set **17**   Worksheet **A**

**Answer each subtraction problem.
Then, check it by addition.**

	A	B	C	D	E	F
1	844 − 579	+	894 − 129	+	794 − 386	+
2	854 − 286	+	654 − 376	+	874 − 652	+
3	744 − 277	+	847 − 472	+	954 − 215	+
4	944 − 158	+	764 − 435	+	964 − 105	+
5	974 − 568	+	940 − 373	+	244 − 87	+
6	344 − 167	+	544 − 249	+	1,044 − 327	+

Math-A-Draw Level III

Name _____ Set **17** Worksheet **B**

To find the hidden picture, draw lines from dot to dot. Follow the order of your answers. Start from the dot with the arrow.

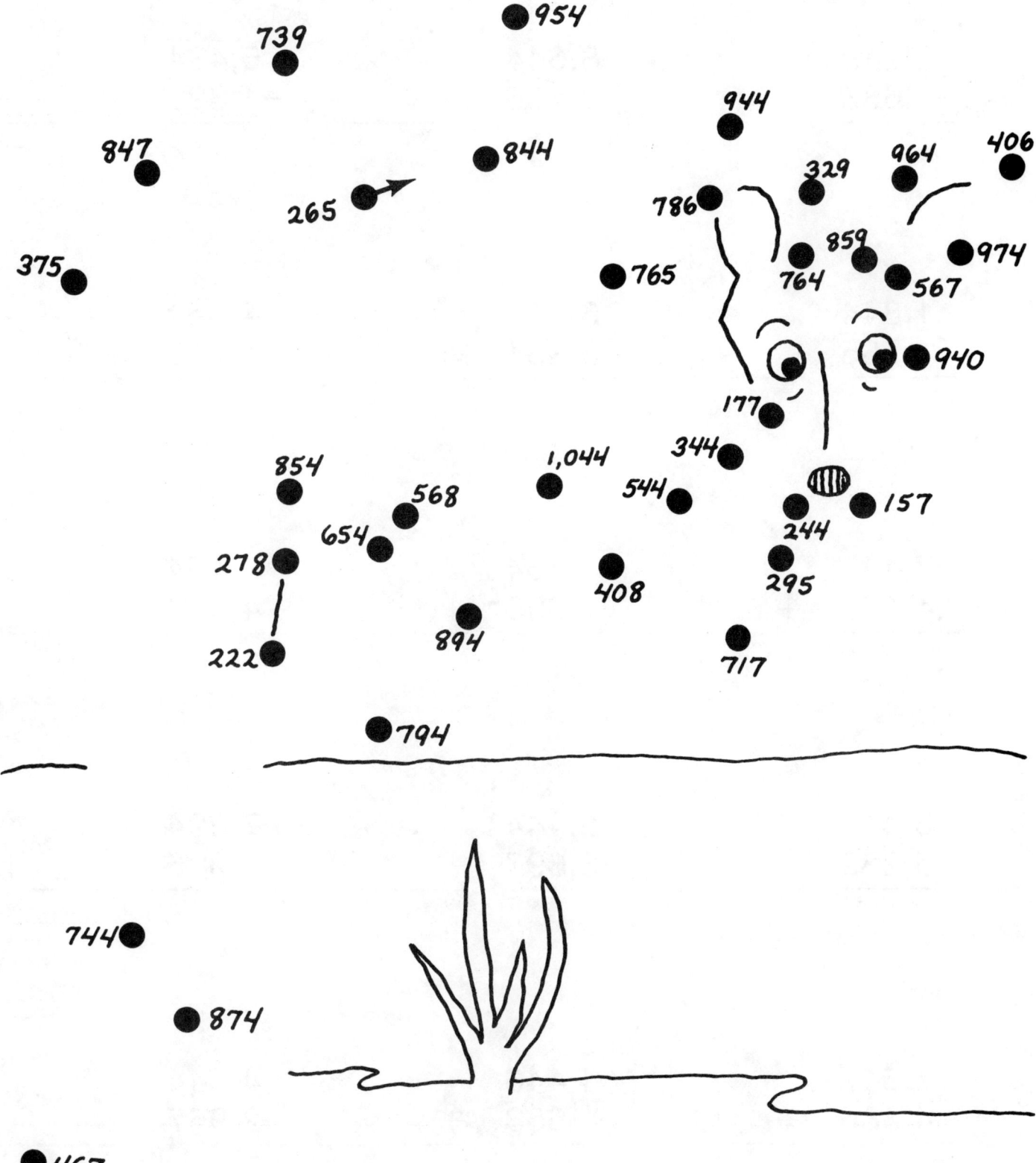

Math-A-Draw Level III

Name _____ Set **18** Worksheet **A**

Answer each subtraction problem.
Then, check it by addition.

	A	B	C	D	E	F
1	2,749 −1,683	+ _____	8,644 −3,486	+ _____	5,434 −4,329	+ _____
2	1,844 − 765	+ _____	6,948 −3,351	+ _____	4,464 − 715	+ _____
3	7,444 −4,157	+ _____	1,454 − 605	+ _____	8,454 −4,526	+ _____
4	8,444 −5,239	+ _____	5,444 −3,397	+ _____	7,294 −5,086	+ _____
5	7,547 −4,386	+ _____	4,446 − 653	+ _____	4,344 −2,967	+ _____

Math-A-Draw Level III

Name _____   Set **18** Worksheet **B**

To find the hidden picture, draw lines from dot to dot. Follow the order of your answers. Start from the dot with the arrow.

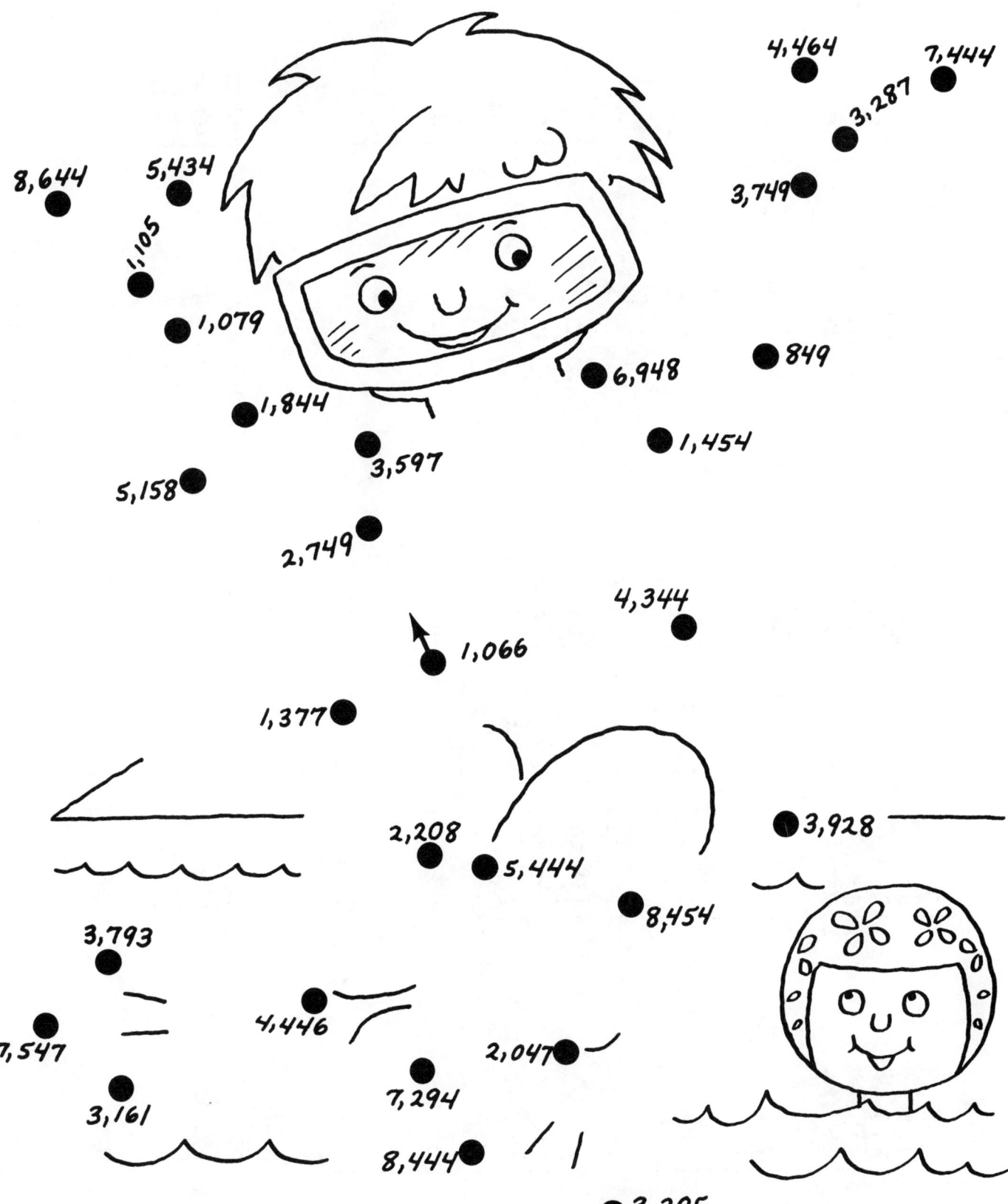

Math-A-Draw Level III

Set 19   Worksheet **A**

Answer each subtraction problem.
Then, check it by addition.

	A	B	C	D	E	F
1	8,446 − 870	+ _____	9,444 − 667	+ _____	8,435 −7,924	+ _____
2	1,844 − 277	+ _____	9,464 −8,958	+ _____	8,445 −6,873	+ _____
3	7,444 −6,881	+ _____	5,648 −5,051	+ _____	8,644 −2,048	+ _____
4	3,482 −2,941	+ _____	6,474 −5,869	+ _____	8,849 − 253	+ _____
5	8,434 −7,986	+ _____	6,349 −4,567	+ _____	7,344 −5,397	+ _____

Math-A-Draw Level III

Name _____ Set **19** Worksheet **B**

To find the hidden picture, draw lines from dot to dot. Follow the order of your answers. Start from the dot with the arrow.

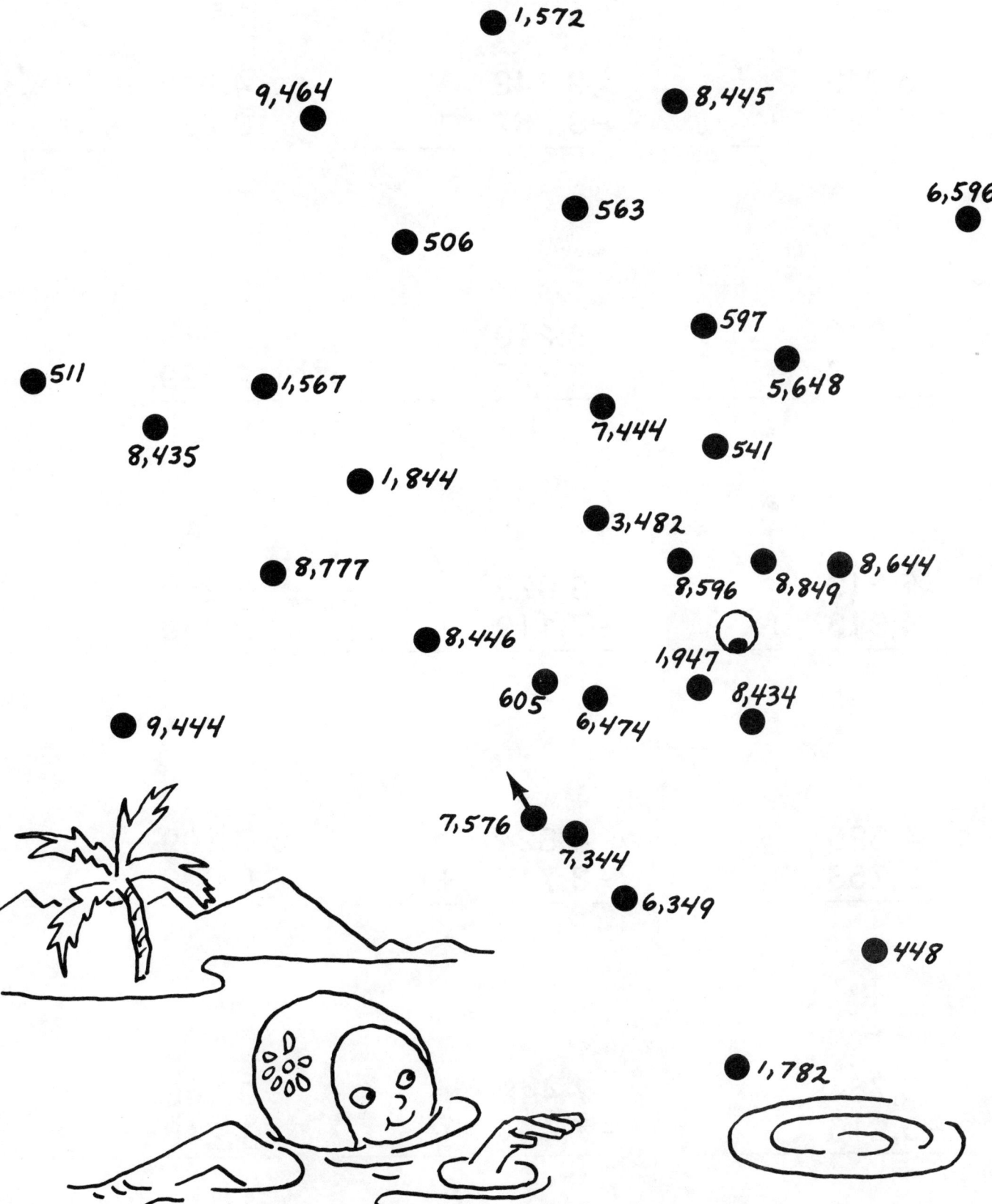

Math-A-Draw Level III

Name _____

Answer each subtraction problem. Then, check it by addition.

Set **20** Worksheet **A**
Review: Subtraction from 10, 11, 12, 13, and 14.

	A	B	C	D	E	F
1	6,043 −5,829	+	9,143 −8,267	+	4,213 −3,238	+
2	4,090 − 87	+	8,210 −5,736	+	5,314 −2,529	+
3	5,210 −4,313	+	8,072 −7,119	+	3,240 −2,786	+
4	4,320 −2,753	+	4,824 −3,713	+	7,109 −6,620	+
5	8,764 −5,216	+	7,442 −7,434	+	2,143 −1,248	+

Math-A-Draw Level III

Name _____ Set **20** Worksheet **B**

To find the hidden picture, draw lines from dot to dot. Follow the order of your answers. Start from the dot with the arrow.

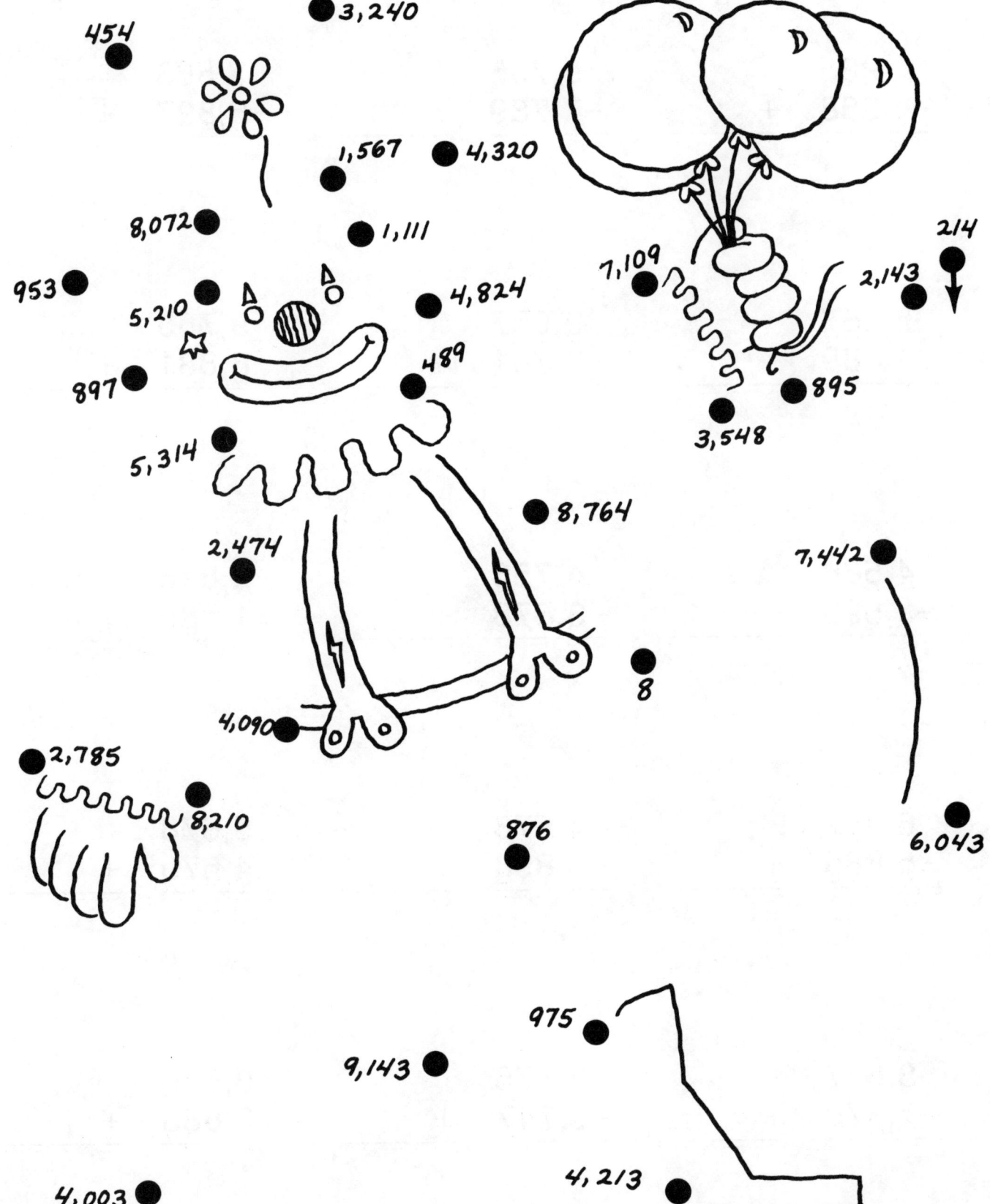

Math-A-Draw Level III

Name _____ Set **21** Worksheet **A**

**Answer each subtraction problem.
Then, check it by addition.**

	A	B	C	D	E	F
1	985 − 888	+ _____	8,765 −7,789	+ _____	7,565 −6,897	+ _____
2	5,657 − 89	+ _____	9,657 −8,761	+ _____	9,755 −8,881	+ _____
3	4,568 − 590	+ _____	4,756 −3,878	+ _____	2,876 −1,889	+ _____
4	6,857 −5,889	+ _____	4,576 −3,898	+ _____	5,678 −4,679	+ _____
5	8,677 −7,779	+ _____	9,576 −8,717	+ _____	9,856 −8,883	+ _____

Math-A-Draw Level III

Name _____ Set **21** Worksheet **B**

To find the hidden picture, draw lines from dot to dot. Follow the order of your answers. Start from the dot with the arrow.

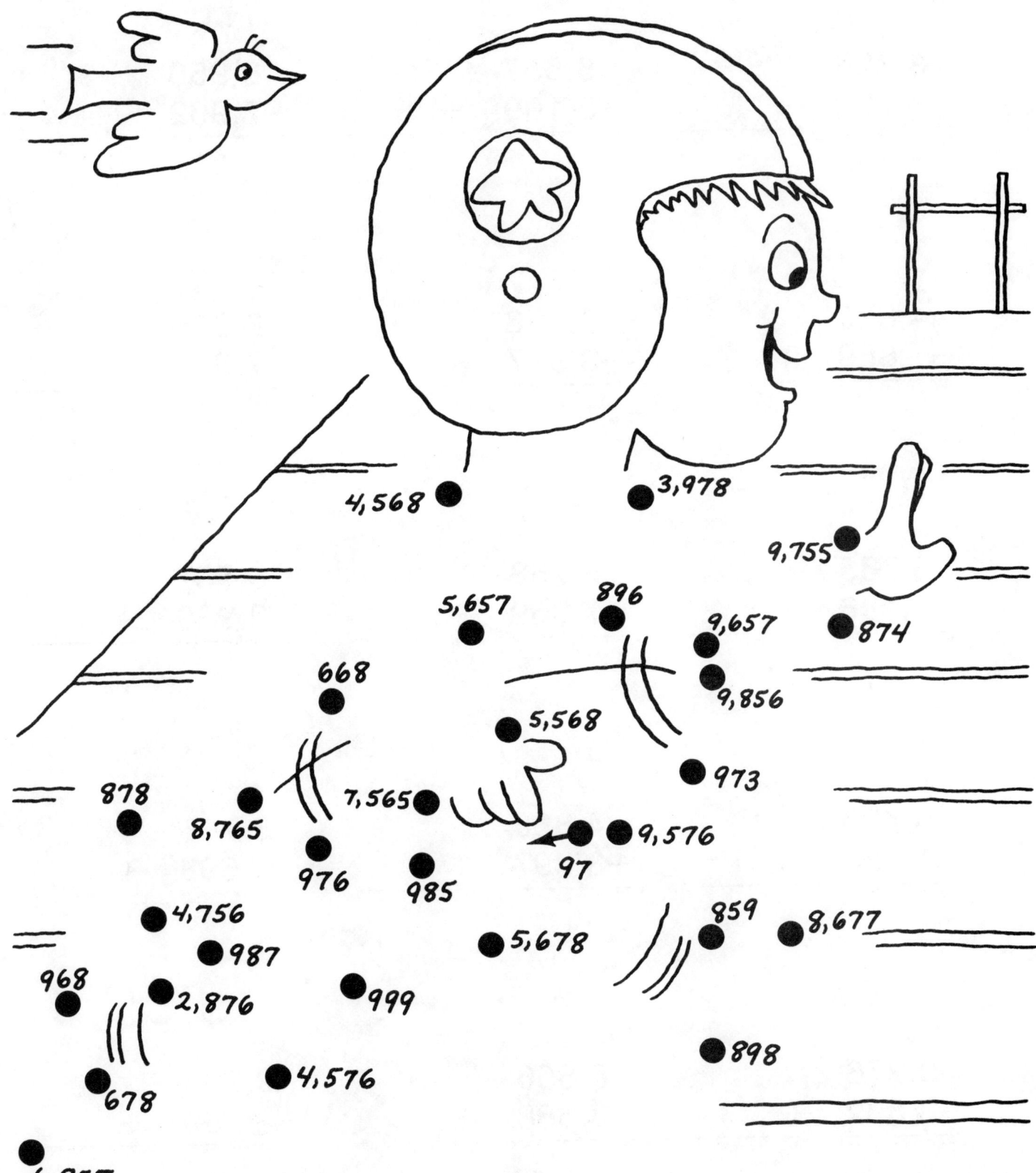

Math-A-Draw Level III

Name _____   Set 22   Worksheet **A**

**Answer each subtraction problem.
Then, check it by addition.**

	A	B	C	D	E	F
1	3,786 − 799	+ _____	8,657 −5,109	+ _____	8,950 −7,962	+ _____
2	4,876 − 889	+ _____	4,756 −3,977	+ _____	8,325 −7,957	+ _____
3	5,785 −3,996	+ _____	8,758 −7,969	+ _____	8,567 −2,989	+ _____
4	5,786 −4,983	+ _____	4,856 −3,897	+ _____	5,765 − 698	+ _____
5	9,876 −3,899	+ _____	8,656 −3,688	+ _____	9,768 − 99	+ _____

Math-A-Draw Level III

Name _____   Set **22** Worksheet **B**

To find the hidden picture, draw lines from dot to dot. Follow the order of your answers. Start from the dot with the arrow.

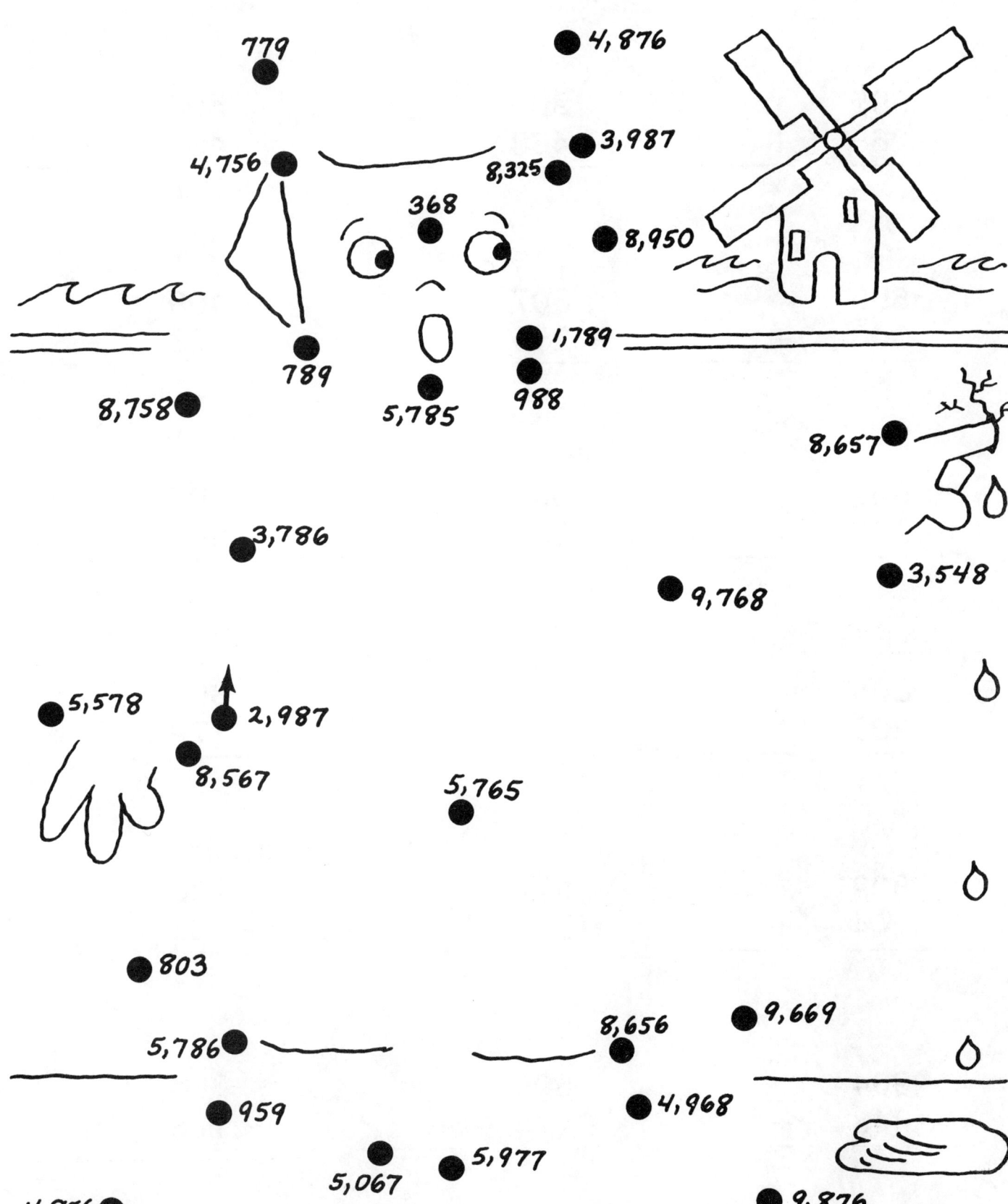

Math-A-Draw Level III

Name _____   Set **23**   Worksheet **A**

Answer each subtraction problem.
Then, check it by addition.

	A	B	C	D	E	F
1	905 − 68	+	901 − 468	+	506 − 497	+
2	505 − 308	+	807 − 259	+	409 − 33	+
3	902 − 365	+	605 − 259	+	906 − 549	+
4	808 − 209	+	401 − 184	+	803 − 179	+
5	809 − 44	+	870 − 595	+	708 − 437	+
6	904 − 848	+	606 − 478	+	604 − 178	+

Math-A-Draw Level III

Name _____   Set **23** Worksheet **B**

To find the hidden picture, draw lines from dot to dot. Follow the order of your answers. Start from the dot with the arrow.

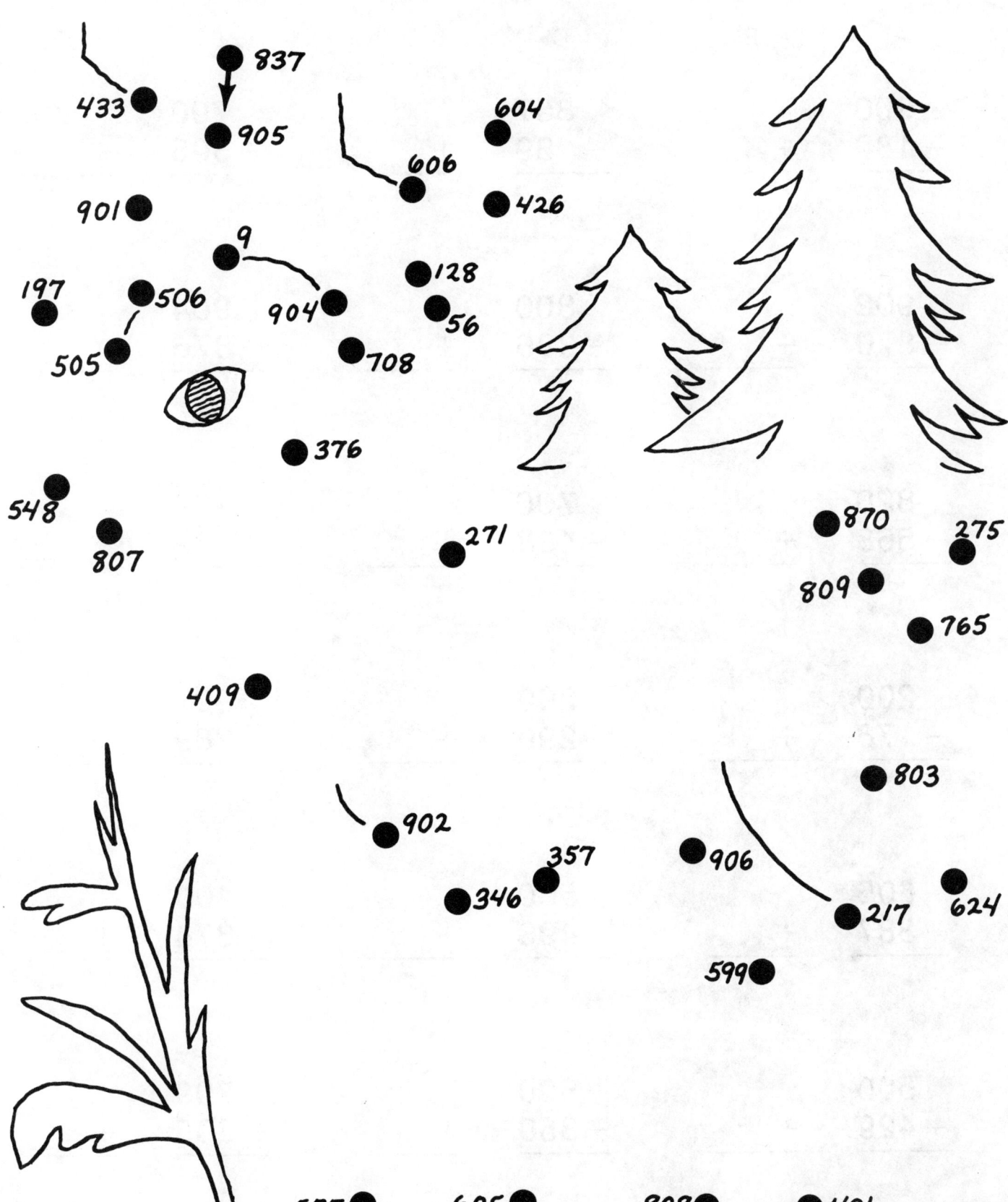

Math-A-Draw Level III

Name _____   Set 24   Worksheet **A**

Answer each subtraction problem.
Then, check it by addition.

	A	B	C	D	E	F
1	900 − 180	+	807 − 39	+	700 − 505	+
2	902 − 870	+	800 − 386	+	904 − 876	+
3	820 − 568	+	706 − 498	+	100 − 79	+
4	200 − 176	+	300 − 290	+	307 − 289	+
5	605 − 387	+	560 − 493	+	400 − 374	+
6	500 − 429	+	600 − 350	+	709 − 305	+

Math-A-Draw Level III

Name _____ Set **24** Worksheet **B**

To find the hidden picture, draw lines from dot to dot. Follow the order of your answers. Start from the dot with the arrow.

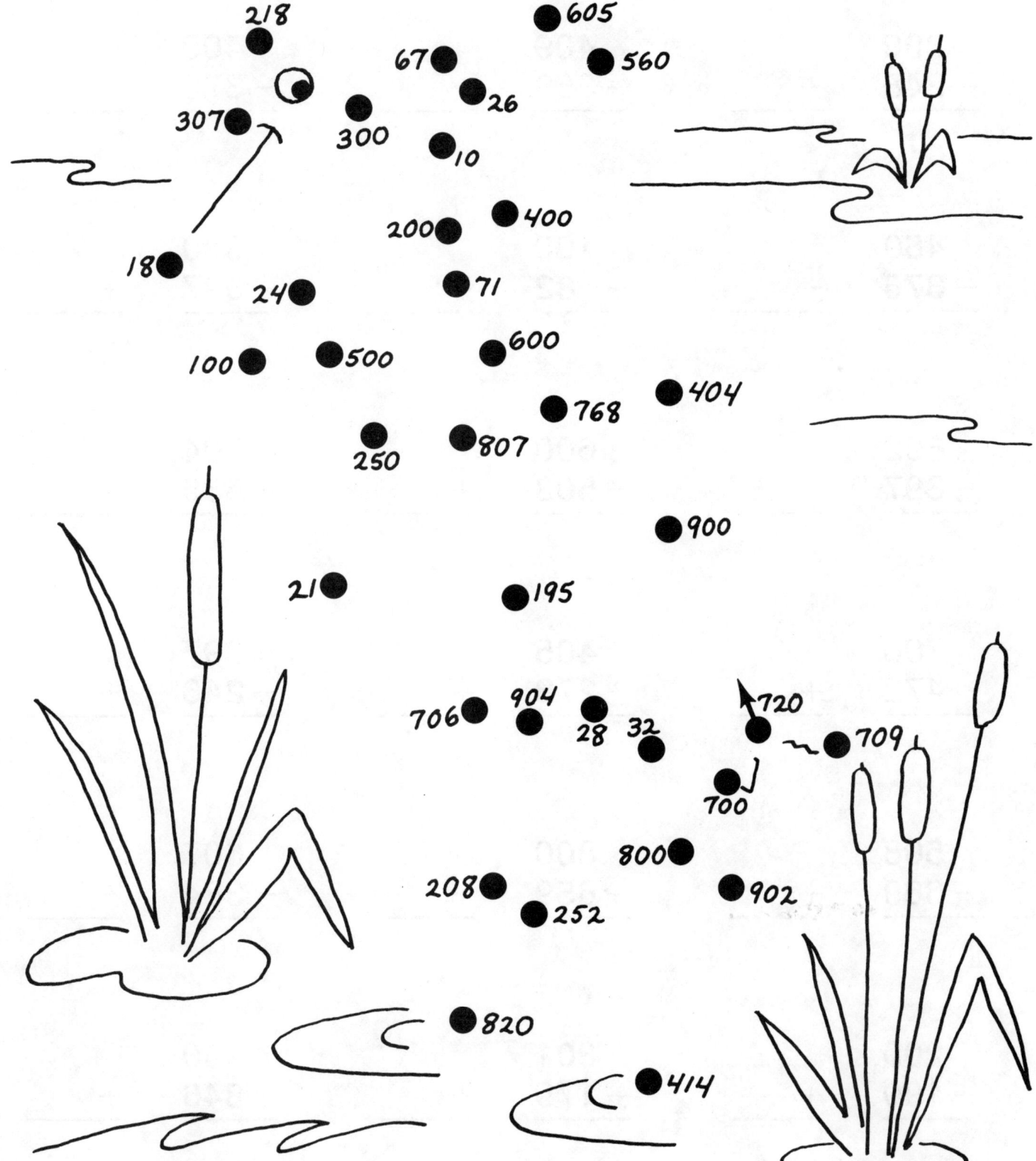

Math-A-Draw Level III

Name _____ Set **25** Worksheet **A**

**Answer each subtraction problem.
Then, check it by addition.**

	A	B	C	D	E	F
1	300 −248	+	409 −368	+	400 −370	+
2	480 −376	+	100 − 82	+	500 −397	+
3	602 −397	+	600 −503	+	704 −685	+
4	700 −472	+	405 −278	+	397 −246	+
5	508 −369	+	800 −659	+	607 −384	+
6	200 −190	+	301 −179	+	900 −846	+

Math-A-Draw Level III

Name _____ Set **25** Worksheet **B**

To find the hidden picture, draw lines from dot to dot. Follow the order of your answers. Start from the dot with the arrow.

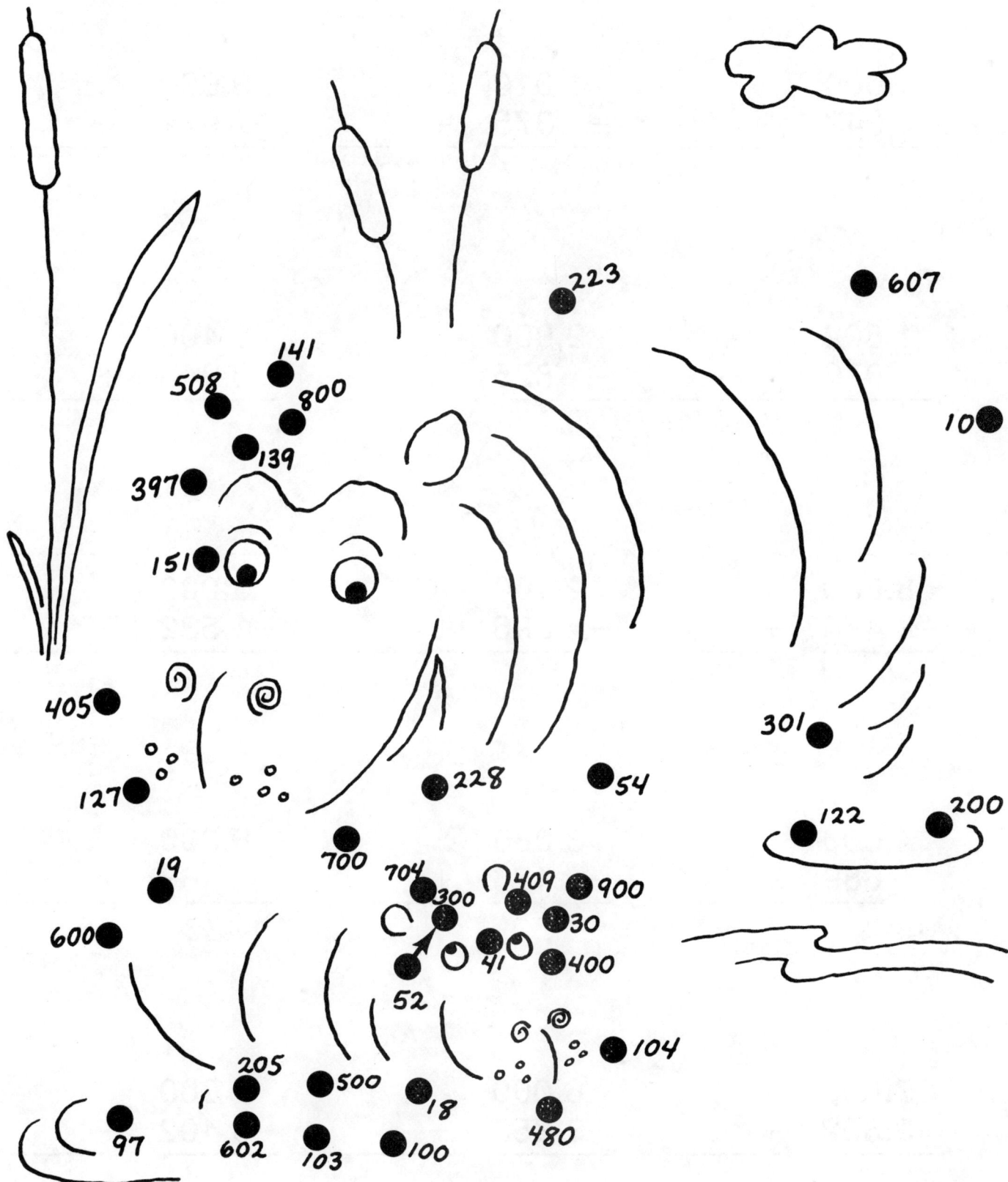

Math-A-Draw Level III

Name _____   Set **26**   Worksheet **A**

**Answer each subtraction problem.
Then, check it by addition.**

	A	B	C	D	E	F
1	1,000 − 547 ─────	+ ─────	1,010 − 375 ─────	+ ─────	9,000 − 972 ─────	+ ─────
2	1,502 − 876 ─────	+ ─────	2,000 − 825 ─────	+ ─────	3,406 −2,943 ─────	+ ─────
3	8,000 − 476 ─────	+ ─────	2,100 − 396 ─────	+ ─────	3,000 −1,532 ─────	+ ─────
4	4,000 − 689 ─────	+ ─────	3,080 − 476 ─────	+ ─────	5,000 − 468 ─────	+ ─────
5	7,065 −3,892 ─────	+ ─────	6,000 −3,358 ─────	+ ─────	7,000 −6,402 ─────	+ ─────

Math-A-Draw Level III

Name _____ Set **26** Worksheet **B**

To find the hidden picture, draw lines from dot to dot. Follow the order of your answers. Start from the dot with the arrow.

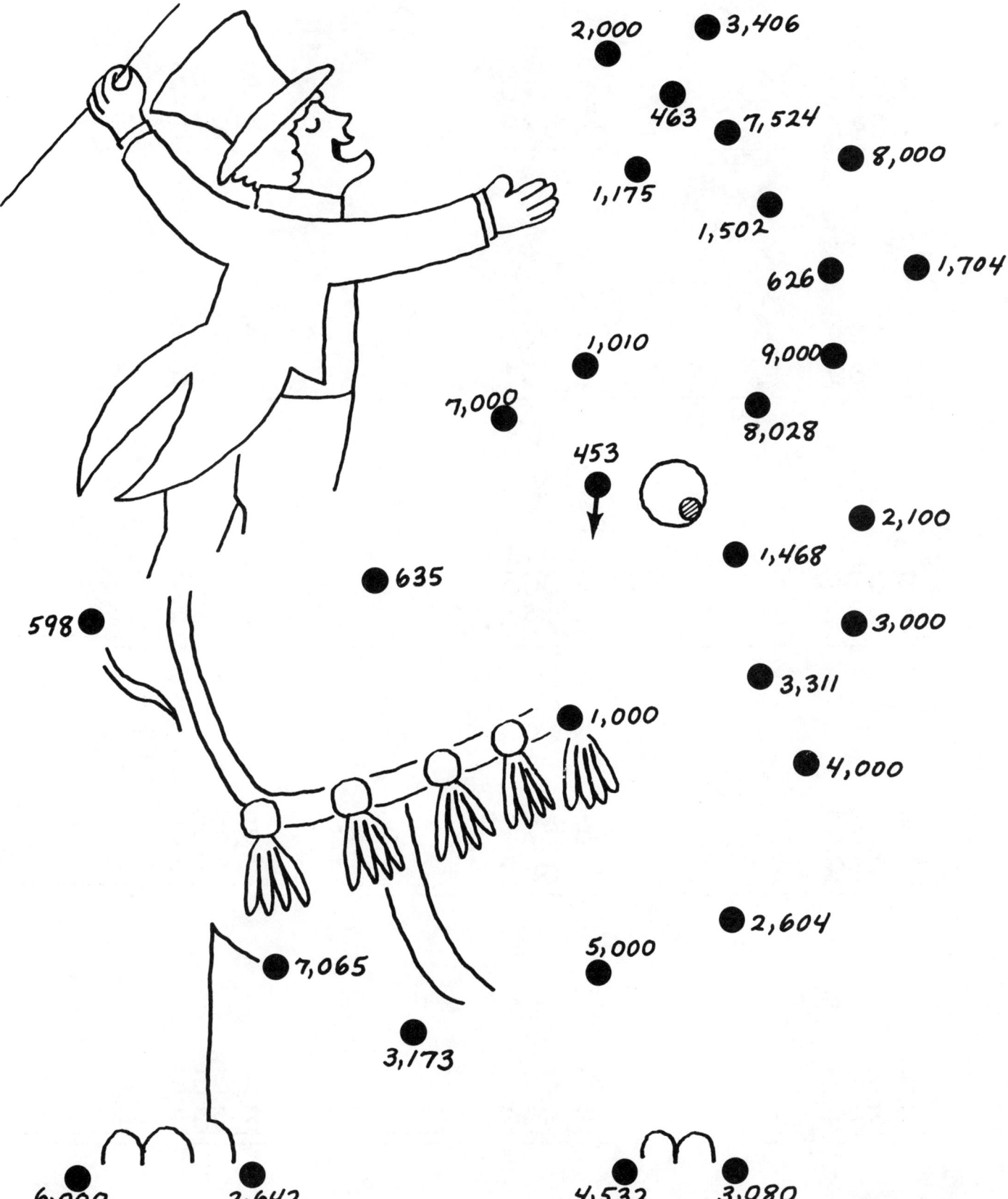

Math-A-Draw Level III

Name _____   Set **27**   Worksheet **A**

**Answer each subtraction problem.
Then, check it by addition.**

	A	B	C	D	E	F
1	9,086 −4,847	+	5,010 −3,879	+	5,000 −4,276	+
2	7,109 − 489	+	9,576 −8,751	+	4,800 − 976	+
3	9,074 −3,727	+	8,005 −5,789	+	9,568 −1,599	+
4	7,080 −3,999	+	8,675 − 988	+	6,000 −3,850	+
5	8,567 −7,699	+	8,000 −6,500	+	9,089 −5,900	+

Math-A-Draw Level III

Name _____   Set **27** Worksheet **B**

To find the hidden picture, draw lines from dot to dot. Follow the order of your answers. Start from the dot with the arrow.

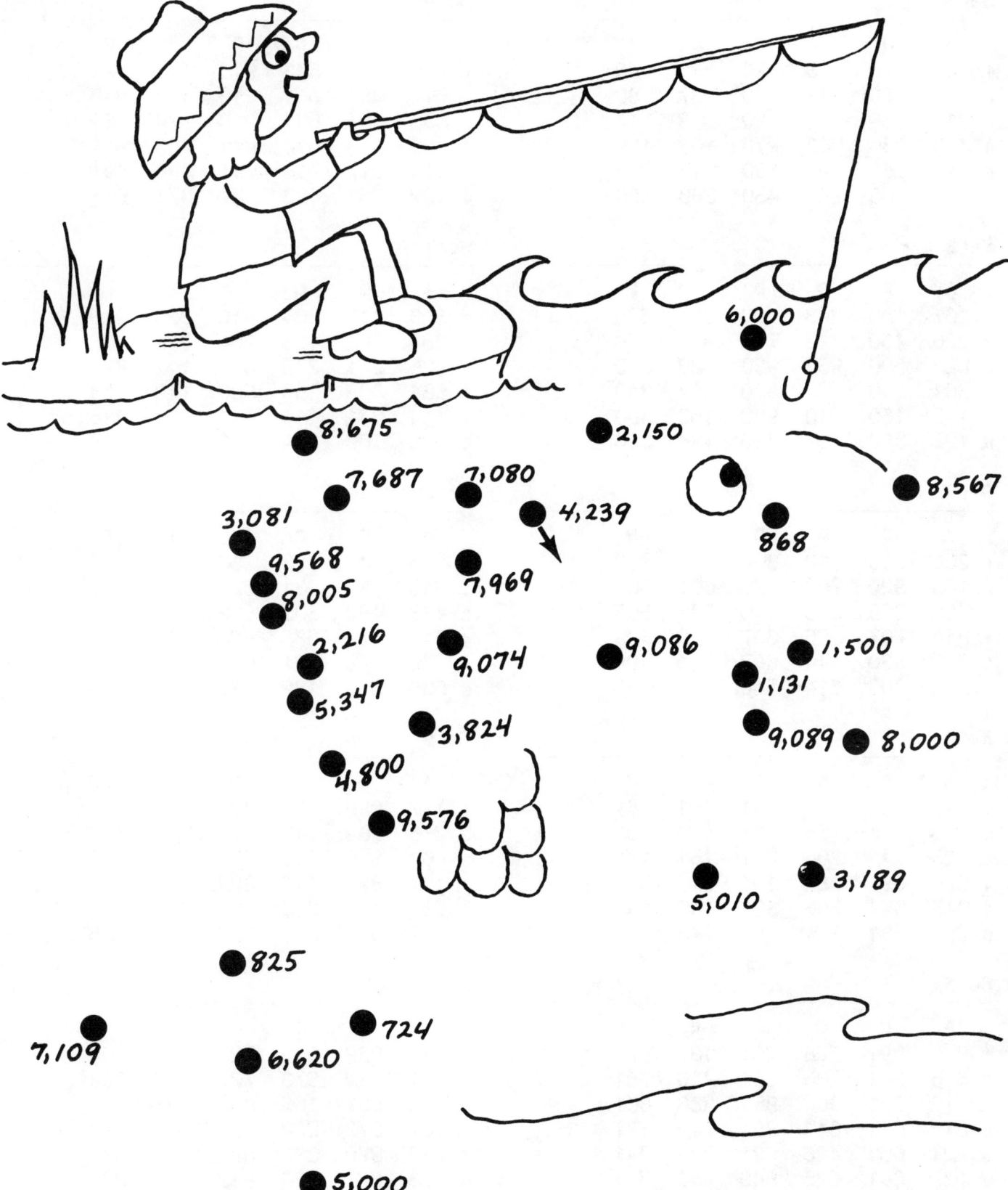

Math-A-Draw Level III

Answer Key

Set 1

	A	B	C	D	E	F
1.	66	70	8	20	11	40
2.	21	60	12	30	37	80
3.	17	50	1	90	3	10
4.	315	350	208	270	103	190
5.	241	250	322	380	217	260
6.	110	150	246	450	263	390

Set 2

	A	B	C	D	E	F
1.	107	180	203	780	312	580
2.	220	450	112	770	307	320
3.	622	690	954	990	420	840
4.	301	640	223	670	317	340
5.	115	160	510	930	153	480
6.	127	350	702	720	124	390

Set 3

	A	B	C	D	E	F
1.	220	300	10	800	441	806
2.	105	920	200	720	601	660
3.	53	808	613	640	131	509
4.	244	707	585	807	333	409
5.	206	530	114	307	141	490
6.	616	709	514	540	740	990

Set 4

	A	B	C	D	E	F
1.	48	51	75	81	1	61
2.	5	71	35	91	10	31
3.	25	41	206	221	151	181
4.	626	691	383	391	547	571
5.	316	341	306	321	106	191
6.	677	681	311	351	745	781

Set 5

	A	B	C	D	E	F
1.	942	991	728	761	137	971
2.	615	941	206	361	416	751
3.	16	821	908	961	329	861
4.	316	871	847	851	215	571
5.	221	651	426	891	733	741
6.	129	841	625	946	6	771

Set 6

	A	B	C	D	E	F
1.	732	814	593	915	103	121
2.	512	951	551	919	393	816
3.	853	881	821	918	24	431
4.	80	413	614	841	403	941
5.	860	917	715	791	236	491
6.	422	751	423	831	371	615

Set 7

	A	B	C	D	E	F
1.	550	813	304	410	326	819
2.	264	708	103	690	372	408
3.	309	911	273	806	111	891
4.	834	905	256	580	110	913
5.	114	341	414	431	721	816
6.	623	709	354	999	622	718

Set 8

	A	B	C	D	E	F
1.	35	42	23	32	313	342
2.	643	725	731	821	642	723
3.	433	462	803	832	307	322
4.	512	522	535	629	724	742
5.	72	128	491	526	334	425
6.	635	982	182	529	81	329

Set 9

	A	B	C	D	E	F
1.	117	922	54	429	123	852
2.	216	782	142	526	311	827
3.	61	629	282	927	132	726
4.	71	829	116	322	712	722
5.	531	622	313	822	332	427
6.	261	821	284	326	32	825

Set 10

	A	B	C	D	E	F
1.	346	832	213	722	105	752
2.	141	422	373	727	463	928
3.	63	932	165	432	637	982
4.	207	972	232	822	43	332
5.	770	829	223	622	26	522
6.	153	322	126	922	127	222

Math-A-Draw Level III

Set 11

	A	B	C	D	E	F
1.	111	509	882	927	318	491
2.	723	790	308	832	511	605
3.	242	727	337	829	30	914
4.	405	690	500	808	292	426
5.	204	481	74	709	519	982
6.	112	437	945	992	664	729

Set 12

	A	B	C	D	E	F
1.	204	763	406	493	48	743
2.	212	749	451	536	214	643
3.	56	933	107	893	707	863
4.	148	843	388	443	853	939
5.	60	938	454	543	176	243
6.	58	343	64	943	237	473

Set 13

	A	B	C	D	E	F
1.	628	883	142	833	299	633
2.	106	723	118	863	367	943
3.	112	634	136	733	158	623
4.	71	532	45	843	44	739
5.	107	613	67	743	175	643
6.	43	435	347	543	36	233

Set 14

	A	B	C	D	E	F
1.	2,851	9,337	556	9,333	737	8,432
2.	2,352	8,338	1,774	5,233	2,843	9,438
3.	1,444	4,339	3,155	8,633	744	6,443
4.	415	4,343	452	3,437	2,103	5,832
5.	424	6,389	631	5,329	1,757	3,443

Set 15

	A	B	C	D	E	F
1.	1,219	4,093	3,555	9,233	7,634	8,231
2.	2,204	8,047	813	6,310	185	3,143
3.	582	4,038	211	7,893	1,541	8,137
4.	4,965	5,393	756	9,832	2,062	7,940
5.	3,343	8,295	1,416	4,309	5,677	6,429

Set 16

	A	B	C	D	E	F
1.	1,761	7,436	3,432	9,695	3,094	8,937
2.	2,893	4,309	5,878	7,940	5,497	6,310
3.	2,874	4,093	2,133	9,389	597	8,231
4.	5,678	9,233	4,965	5,393	2,968	3,143
5.	4,952	8,295	6,596	8,137	5,842	8,047

Set 17

	A	B	C	D	E	F
1.	265	844	765	894	408	794
2.	568	854	278	654	222	874
3.	467	744	375	847	739	954
4.	786	944	329	764	859	964
5.	406	974	567	940	157	244
6.	177	344	295	544	717	1,044

Set 18

	A	B	C	D	E	F
1.	1,066	2,749	5,158	8,644	1,105	5,434
2.	1,079	1,844	3,597	6,948	3,749	4,464
3.	3,287	7,444	849	1,454	3,928	8,454
4.	3,205	8,444	2,047	5,444	2,208	7,294
5.	3,161	7,547	3,793	4,446	1,377	4,344

Set 19

	A	B	C	D	E	F
1.	7,576	8,446	8,777	9,444	511	8,435
2.	1,567	1,844	506	9,464	1,572	8,445
3.	563	7,444	597	5,648	6,596	8,644
4.	541	3,482	605	6,474	8,596	8,849
5.	448	8,434	1,782	6,349	1,947	7,344

Set 20

	A	B	C	D	E	F
1.	214	6,043	876	9,143	975	4,213
2.	4,003	4,090	2,474	8,210	2,785	5,314
3.	897	5,210	953	8,072	454	3,240
4.	1,567	4,320	1,111	4,824	489	7,109
5.	3,548	8,764	8	7,442	895	2,143

Set 21

	A	B	C	D	E	F
1.	97	985	976	8,765	668	7,565
2.	5,568	5,657	896	9,657	874	9,755
3.	3,978	4,568	878	4,756	987	2,876
4.	968	6,857	678	4,576	999	5,678
5.	898	8,677	859	9,576	973	9,856

Set 22

	A	B	C	D	E	F
1.	2,987	3,786	3,548	8,657	988	8,950
2.	3,987	4,876	779	4,756	368	8,325
3.	1,789	5,785	789	8,758	5,578	8,567
4.	803	5,786	959	4,856	5,067	5,765
5.	5,977	9,876	4,968	8,656	9,669	9,768

Set 23

	A	B	C	D	E	F
1.	837	905	433	901	9	506
2.	197	505	548	807	376	409
3.	537	902	346	605	357	906
4.	599	808	217	401	624	803
5.	765	809	275	870	271	708
6.	56	904	128	606	426	604

Set 24

	A	B	C	D	E	F
1.	720	900	768	807	195	700
2.	32	902	414	800	28	904
3.	252	820	208	706	21	100
4.	24	200	10	300	18	307
5.	218	605	67	560	26	400
6.	71	500	250	600	404	709

Set 25

	A	B	C	D	E	F
1.	52	300	41	409	30	400
2.	104	480	18	100	103	500
3.	205	602	97	600	19	704
4.	228	700	127	405	151	397
5.	139	508	141	800	223	607
6.	10	200	122	301	54	900

Set 26

	A	B	C	D	E	F
1.	453	1,000	635	1,010	8,028	9,000
2.	626	1,502	1,175	2,000	463	3,406
3.	7,524	8,000	1,704	2,100	1,468	3,000
4.	3,311	4,000	2,604	3,080	4,532	5,000
5.	3,173	7,065	2,642	6,000	598	7,000

Set 27

	A	B	C	D	E	F
1.	4,239	9,086	1,131	5,010	724	5,000
2.	6,620	7,109	825	9,576	3,824	4,800
3.	5,347	9,074	2,216	8,005	7,969	9,568
4.	3,081	7,080	7,687	8,675	2,150	6,000
5.	868	8,567	1,500	8,000	3,189	9,089

Math-A-Draw Level III

THIS IS

MATH·A·DRAW RECORD.

1	2	3
4	5	6
7	8	9
10	11	12
13	14	15
16	17	18
19	20	21
22	23	24
25	26	27

Congratulations

_____

for excellence in
MATH·A·DRAW

_____
TEACHER

_____
DATE

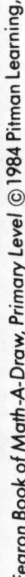

Math-A-Draw Level III